HINDUISM
WORLD RELIGIONS

by
Madhu Bazaz Wangu

Facts On File
An imprint of Infobase Publishing

HINDUISM, THIRD EDITION
World Religions

Copyright © 2006, 2001, 1991 by Madhu Bazaz Wangu

Facts On File, Inc.
An Imprint of Infobase Publishing
132 West 31st Street
New York NY 10001

Library of Congress Cataloging-in-Publication Data
Wangu, Madhu Bazaz.
    Hinduism / by Madhu Bazaz Wangu. — 3rd ed.
      p. cm. — (World religions)
    Includes index.
    ISBN 0-8160-6611-6
    1. Hinduism—Juvenile literature. I. Title. II. Series.
BL1203.W35 2006
294.5--dc22

2006044573

Facts On File books are available at special discounts when purchased in bulk quantities for businesses, associations, institutions or sales promotions. Please contact the Special Sales Department in New York at 212/967-8800 or 800/322-8755.

You can find Facts On File on the World Wide Web at http://www.factsonfile.com

Developed by Brown Publishing Network, Inc. Design Production by Jennifer Angell/ Brown Publishing Network, Inc. Photo Research by Sue McDermott

Photo credits:

Cover: Getty Images; *Title page:* Morning prayers in the Ganges, John Henebry; *Table of Contents:* Shiva Nataraga, Delhi National Museum, Giradoun/Art Resource, NY; *Pages 6–7:* John Henebry; *11:* John Henebry; *12:* Madhu Bazaz Wangu; *14–15:* Robert & Linda Mitchell; *17:* ACSAA slide " AAAUM; *19:* John Henebry; *24–25:* John Henebry; *27:* Ken Laffal; *34:* Ross-Coomaraswamy Collection, courtesy, Museum of Fine Arts, Boston; *39:* John Henebry; *42–43:* ACSAA slide " AAAUM; *44:* By courtesy of the Board of Trustees of the Victoria & Albert Museum; *55:* John Henebry; *58:* ACSAA slide " AAAUM; *62:* Madhu Bazaz Wangu; *68–69:* AP/Wide World; *72:* John A. Henebry; *76:* AP/Wide World; *84–85:* SEF/Art Resource, NY; *88:* Clemens Kalischer; *93:* John Henebry; *94:* Reuters/Bettmann; *97:* Clemens Kalischer; *100–101:* Madhu Bazaz Wangu; *110:* (*left*) John Henebry; *110:* (*right*) Robert & Linda Mitchell; *112:* Madhu Bazaz Wangu; *116–117:* UPI/Bettmann; *121:* UPI/Bettmann; *122:* BAPS Swaminarayan Sanstha

Printed in the United States of America

10 9 8 7 6 5 4 3 2 1

This book is printed on acid-free paper

TABLE OF CONTENTS

Preface

Our present era is sometimes called a "secular age," meaning, in effect, that religion is not an especially important issue for most people. But there is much evidence to suggest that this is not true. In many societies, including the United States, religion and religious values shape the lives of millions of individuals and play a key role in politics and culture as well.

The World Religions series, of which this book is a part, is designed to appeal to both students and general readers. The books offer clear, accessible overviews of the major religious traditions and institutions of our time. Each volume in the series describes where a particular religion is practiced, its origins and history, its central beliefs and important rituals, and its contributions to world civilization. Carefully chosen photographs complement the text, and a glossary and bibliography are included to help readers gain a more complete understanding of the subject at hand.

Religious institutions and spirituality have always played a central role in world history. These books will help clarify what religion is all about and reveal both the similarities and differences in the great spiritual traditions practiced around the world today.

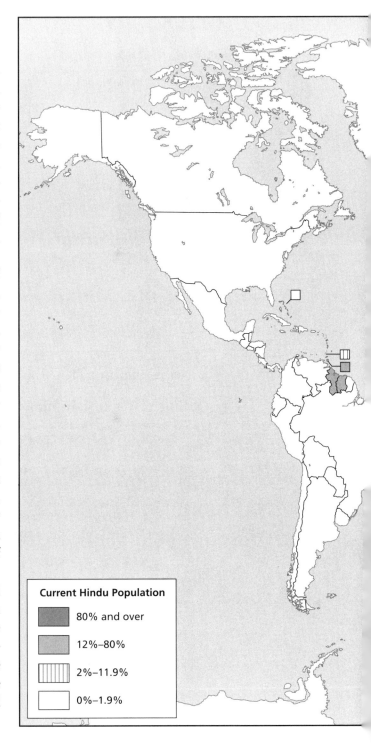

Current Hindu Population

- 80% and over
- 12%–80%
- 2%–11.9%
- 0%–1.9%

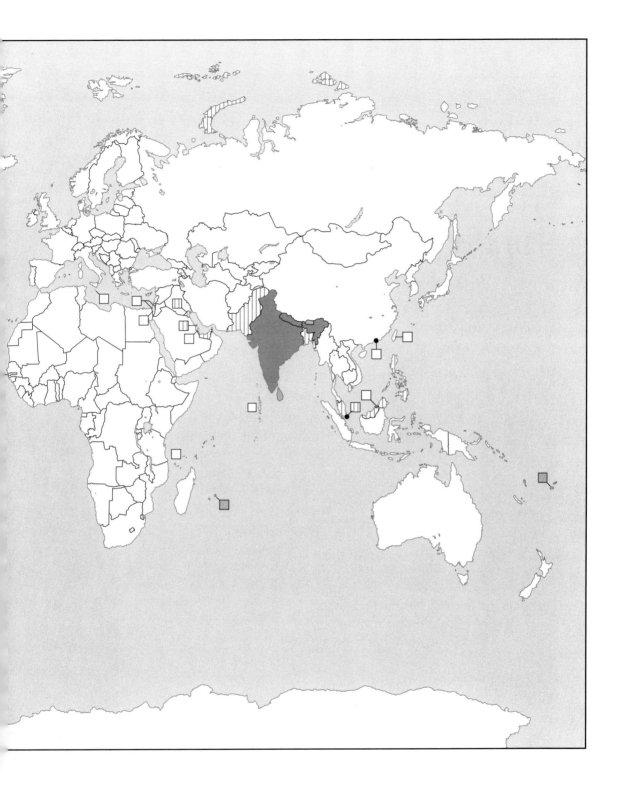

CHAPTER 1

Introduction: The Modern Hindu World

*H*induism is one of the oldest religions in existence. After Christianity and Islam, it ranks as the world's third-largest religion. Today, there are about 837 million Hindus worldwide.

The majority of Hindus live in India, where the religion was born. Nepal, the only officially Hindu country in the world, is the nation with the highest percentage of Hindus, 89 percent. There are also significant Hindu minorities in Bangladesh and Indonesia, and smaller groups can be found in Sri Lanka, Pakistan, Fiji, Guyana, Africa, Great Britain, Canada, and the United States. While Hindus in each of these societies have altered their religion to suit the needs of their cultures, all Hindus share a core of rich, poetic, and complex traditions.

Unlike Buddhism, Confucianism, Taoism, Christianity, Islam, or most of the other active world religions, Hinduism was not founded by one individual. Rather, it is the result of a coming together of many religious beliefs and philosophical schools. The different schools of thought and doctrine that flourished on Indian soil over the centuries were not originally labeled as Hindu. Nor was there a religion called Hinduism. The name *Hindu* came into use when the Persians, in their attempt to label all

6   HINDUISM: World Religions

non-Muslim people living beyond the Sindhu River, mispronounced the word *Sindhu.*

In later centuries, Arabs, Turks, Afghans, and Mughals—all Muslims—used the term *Hindu* just for the sake of convenience. In their view of the world, there were the believers of Islam and "the rest." Hindus were, therefore, "the rest," and Hinduism was considered to be the religion of all non-Muslims. It is important to note that all of those who were grouped together as "the rest" were not Hindus. As mentioned, Hinduism was a particular religion that gradually developed among many of the non-Muslims.

Early Hinduism combined the religions of the Indus Valley in northwestern India with that of Aryan invaders from Persia. Later, Hinduism developed a more solid foundation through the writing and interpretation of the great Hindu scriptures. Throughout its many years, Hinduism has also developed as a result of the challenges of foreigners. India found itself conquered and ruled repeatedly by foreign invaders—Arabs, Turks, Afghans, Mughals, and the British. The unique cultures and religions of these invaders have had an effect on the ideas and principles of Hinduism. Yet, despite these many influences and the changes that came to pass, India has remained essentially Hindu.

The Gods and the Scriptures

From its beginnings, Hinduism has been a polytheistic religion, meaning that its followers believe in many gods. Some people estimate the number of Hindu gods to be in the thousands. Others suggest that though innumerable minor gods exist, there is really only one true "god" at the heart of Hinduism—*Brahman.* Brahman is also called the One, the Ultimate Reality, and the World Soul. According to this interpretation, the many gods traditionally found in Hinduism really form part of Brahman.

The Hindus have come to know about their many gods by listening to and reading an enormous body of sacred literature. They have never followed the teachings contained in a single holy book, such as the Bible of Judaism and Christianity or the Koran (Qur'an) of Islam. Although at the beginning of the 20th century, Western scholars working on ancient Hindu literature tried to isolate a "Hindu Bible" and believed that they were successful in identifying the Bhagavad Gita as the holy book, more recent scholars recognize that no single text is most important. Hinduism recognizes several sacred writings, all of which contribute to basic Hindu beliefs.

There are two main categories of Hindu scripture—*shruti,* "that which is heard," and *smriti,* "tradition" or "that which is to be remembered." The Vedas and the Upanishads fall into the category of *shruti.* These sacred writings are considered to be inspired by God and to have been revealed to humankind by ancient sages called *rishis.*

Each of the *shruti* texts provides an important part of the foundation of Hinduism. The four Vedas are the oldest of the texts and are the primary scriptures of Hinduism. It is difficult to assign exact dates to these writings, because many were compiled gradually, over centuries, through oral tradition. They were written down only long after they had come into existence. One of the four Vedas contains hymns, chants, and praises to the gods. Another Veda serves as a guidebook for rituals and priestly behavior. A third offers information on magic and charms that can be used as blessings or curses, and the fourth gives musical notes to be chanted while performing the rituals. Together, the four Vedas have had a deep and lasting influence on Hinduism. The Brahmanas were texts composed after the Vedas. These texts give the details of the routines to be followed during the fire sacrifices. Aranyakas "the forest books" composed after the Brahamanas emphasize only the meaning of rituals.

The Upanishads, the latest of the *shruti* scriptures, were written around 700–500 B.C.E. One meaning for the word *Upanishad* is "sitting down near" a *guru* (spiritual master) who passes on his secret teachings. Almost all Upanishads are written in the form of dialogues between a student and a teacher. Indeed, many of the Upanishadic teachings were to become permanent elements of Hinduism. Most important of these are the concepts of *karma* (one's deeds will later have an effect in this life or in another life), *samsara* (reincarnation, or the cycles of a soul's birth and rebirth), and *moksha* (release from the cycles of samsara). In addition, the Upanishads treated questions about the nature of both *atman* (the soul of the individual) and Brahman (the Universal Soul), and their relationship to each other. These questions have played an important role in the development and practice of Hinduism.

Because of their divine origin, *shruti* texts are considered to be more sacred than the other class of scriptures, *smriti*. Works that come after the Vedas and the Upanishads are all *smriti*. These include epics, the *puranas, sutras, shastras,* and devotional *bhakti* songs.

India boasts of two great *smriti* epics. Both of them, the *Mahabharata* and the *Ramayana,* have had a significant influence on Hindu thought. These two epics have had many layers added to them over the centuries, and both have undergone numerous changes.

The *Mahabharata,* containing over 90,000 stanzas, is probably the longest epic poem in history. According to Hindu tradition, the sage Vyasa dictated it to Ganesha, the elephant god of good luck and wisdom and the patron of learning. It tells the story of two families engaged in war. It includes the Bhagavad Gita, an important sacred text in Hinduism that tells an important story about the god Krishna.

The other great epic, the *Ramayana* (The goings of Rama), tells the tale of Rama, the seventh incarnation of the god Vishnu. The *Ramayana* depicts the ideals of faithfulness to marriage vows, brotherly affection, and loyalty. The earliest parts of the text date from around 350 B.C.E., but the work as a whole was not compiled until much later. Both the *Mahabharata* and the *Ramayana* have influenced the philosophy of Hinduism for over two thousand years.

The *Puranas*—literally "something very old"—are also *smriti* writings. Written in Sanskrit, these texts form a collection of verses that tell the stories of Hinduism's best-known gods and goddesses and the lives of ancient heroes. They include creation stories, portraits of the gods and famous sages, and accounts of time periods ruled by semi-gods called *manus*. They also speak of the end of the world and its rebirth, the history of humankind, and the legends of ancient dynasties. The *Puranas* are referred to as the Vedas of the common people, because they present traditional religious and historical material through tales that most Hindus can understand.

Another popular form of scripture is the bhakti literature. These devotional songs were produced in both southern and northern regions of India, where teachers emphasized the love of those devoted to a personal god or goddess and the love returned by the god or goddess. The bhakti movement developed a number of poet-sages who sang praises to Hindu gods and goddesses in the languages of the common people. By the sixth century C.E., these devotional hymns were being sung in many temples. Even today, many Hindus write and sing bhakti hymns.

The Hindu scriptures, and the stories they contain, guide Hindus in their daily lives. They also help to preserve the religious dimensions of family and society. From these texts, and from their interpretations, Hindus have developed their system of worship and beliefs.

Hindu Worship and Beliefs

Three major sects comprise Hinduism, each based on a different idea of the divine, the universe, and the human condition. These sects are each represented by a high god—Shiva, Vishnu, or Shakti—and are referred to as Shaivism, Vaishnavism, and Shaktism, respectively. The different sects of Hinduism are loosely bound together by a single belief: they recognize that many different and individual paths may lead to the one ultimate goal of Hinduism, *moksha*, which is release from the attachment people have to this material world. Each sect lays out its own way of attaining *moksha*'s reward—a blissful union with the universal spirit of Brahman.

Some important rituals, beliefs, and traditions keep the religion vital and hold all the sects of Hinduism together. These are *puja*, or daily worship; *dharma*, religious duties pertaining to family and society; *samskara*, rites of passage; samsara, belief in the reincarnation or reappearance of the soul in succeeding generations; and *moksha*, or final release from material existence.

Each day, Hindus worship the divine—either a high god or a family deity. To do this, they perform *puja* in a sacred corner in a worship room of the home. The *puja* ritual keeps Hindus aware of their gods and mindful of their duties as individuals.

The most exalted setting for performing *puja* is the temple. The temple is the house of god and a link between human

■ *People crowd into a small Ganesha shrine. The statue of the god, placed on a high pedestal, overlooks his devotees. In the upper right-hand corner is a large metal bell that devotees ring as they enter the temple.*

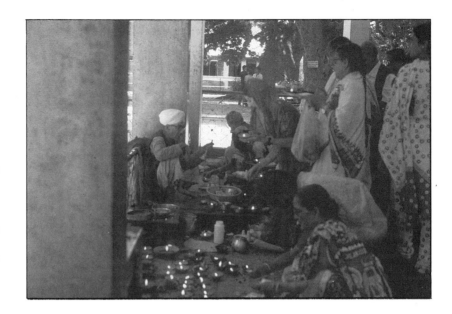

■ *Devotees perform a special kind of ritual, called* **puja,** *which involves all the senses. Lighted earthen lamps evoke the sense of sight; the sound of a bell evokes the sense of hearing; fragrant leaves and flowers evoke the sense of smell; ritual objects evoke the sense of touch; and finally, consumption of blessed food evokes the sense of taste.*

existence and the divine. It is also the center of social, artistic, intellectual, and religious affairs. Most essentially, for a Hindu, the temple is a place of passage from this world to the next.

As early as the Vedic period, Hindu society was roughly divided into four levels based on occupations. This basic part of Hindu life is known as the *caste system.* The Hindu caste system was supported by dharma, early religious laws of duty. Dharma insisted that particular castes had certain duties within the society. An individual, as a member of a caste, was responsible for upholding those duties. To neglect them was considered a sin that would upset the balance of life in the universe. Early Hindus believed, as do many modern Hindus, that if everyone were to perform his or her duty unquestioningly, a balance could be maintained in the world and humans could exist in peace.

More recently, the laws binding people to respect the caste system have been loosened. As a result, modern dharma focuses more on duties to family than to society. Today, the family unit is considered especially sacred, and the fulfillment of obligations to the family is a religious duty.

Within every family and throughout society, individual life is divided into four stages—childhood, youth, middle age, and old age. Hindus practice samskara, traditional rites of passage, to mark these important transitions from the moment of conception to the time of death. All rites of passage, including those of death and afterlife, are performed at home by the head of the household. According to tradition, each family member is responsible for maintaining sacred order in the family, in society, and ultimately in the universe. The celebration of these rites of passage are part of that order. Religious observance of the basic rites (conception and birth, introduction to the guru for initiation, marriage, and cremation after death) are believed to be part of the path that leads Hindus toward their goal of *moksha*.

In their pursuit of *moksha*, Hindus share the ultimate goal of being spiritually united with the Ultimate Reality—Brahman. Thus, Hindus consider the physical world to be unreal and only the world of mind and spirit to be real. To achieve *moksha*, they seek inner peace and harmony in their lives. Hindus believe that all their actions and deeds will have some future effect—either in this life or in a future life of their souls. This idea is called the law of karma, and it governs all Hindu actions.

Because all human efforts and deeds are subject to the law of karma, Hindus try to erase their desires to achieve something in this utilitarian material world. This is because if they focus on achieving something in this material world, they will only prepare themselves for additional rebirths or new lives (samsara) in future generations on earth. Such efforts never lead to release from the material existence of this world. *Moksha* cannot be achieved by action aimed at gaining something in this world but only by an experience of oneself as united with god, the oneness of *atman-Brahman*, the union of one's self with the Ultimate Reality.

As we shall see, Hinduism celebrates sacred human fertility and spiritual and creative power. Gradually, it blossoms into the symbolism of the sacred space of the temple and sensuous worship. Finally, Hinduism thrives, united by its believers' faith that there will come a time for a joining with the Ultimate Reality.

CHAPTER **2**

The Roots of Hinduism

*H*induism was not always the complex religion it is today. It developed gradually, as a merging of the beliefs and practices of two main groups—the people of the Indus Valley in India and the Aryans of Persia. These groups were not actually Hindus. There was no such thing as Hinduism when they existed. Rather, Hinduism later developed from their religious practices, literature, and systems for establishing social order.

Our knowledge of the early stages of Hinduism comes chiefly from archaeological findings and the earliest Hindu scriptures, the Vedas. Archaeological artifacts help us to know about the civilization of the Indus Valley, both before and after the Aryan invasion. They tell about practical matters, but they also tell about spiritual life. Scriptures are the source of the beliefs, rituals, and portraits of the gods of the early Hindus, and they also add to the history of the civilization.

From historical evidence, we know that in this period, early Hindu religious ideas were developed and clarified. Religion was a central part of life in the Indus Valley, and it helped to define the structure of society—the way individuals acted and

interacted. Many of these ideas, both social and religious, still form a part of the basis of Hinduism.

Indus Valley Civilization

About 5,000 years ago, in what is today Pakistan and northwestern India, a lively culture flourished on the banks of the Indus River. The Indus people lived in brick houses in well-planned villages. They were successful food cultivators who raised buffalo, goats, sheep, pigs, and dogs. They also exported cotton. Their comfortable civilization was built on a thriving agricultural and animal economy.

The Indus were governed by a strong ruling class who had much concern for cleanliness, order, and stability. As we know from archaeological findings, personal hygiene and ritual cleanliness were of special importance to the Indus. Each house in an Indus Valley village had a bathing room with drains. Also, there are many remains of bathing areas located in public places.

In one of the major Indus towns, Mohenjo-Daro, was the Great Bath, a principal public structure. It contained a large water tank with entry steps leading downward at each end. Special rooms for private bathing surrounded the tank. Such rooms and a large water tank are still a common feature of modern Hindu temples.

Most information about the religious life of the Indus Valley people comes from the artifacts they have left behind. These include numerous terra-cotta figurines and seals, such as those found by archaeologists in Mohenjo-Daro and another major town, Harappa. These relics provide information about the beliefs of the Indus people as well as their craftsmanship. We know from the seals and figurines that the Indus people honored fertility, sexual power, and certain sacred animals.

It is not certain how the seals from Harappa and Mohenjo-Daro were used. Many of the scenes depicted on the seals relate to the sacredness of sexual power and human creativity. Some scholars have indicated that whatever their use, the seals serve as evidence of the high quality of work produced by the two towns.

The terra-cotta figurines are so numerous that they seem to have been kept in nearly every home. Their craftsmanship is in

■ *Preceding page— Roaming cows are a constant presence in Indian towns and cities. Cows and bulls are sacred, not only because cows provide foods such as milk and cheese, but because cows were Krishna's companions. Bulls have been sacred since the times of the Indus Valley culture. Killing cows and bulls is a sin, and eating beef is sacrilegious.*

■ *This drawing shows the elaborate headdress of an Indus Valley terra-cotta figurine.*

these instances often rather crude when compared to the seals and some other small-scale sculptures found in public buildings of the Indus Valley. Because they are somewhat unrefined, family figurines may have been created by the common people for their own use, rather than by expert craftsmen for use by the upper classes.

The most common types of figurines from this period represent what are often considered to be "mother-goddesses." Almost all of these figures convey some idea of fertility and motherhood. They feature a female with wide hips, small breasts, tubular limbs, abundant jewelry, and an elaborate headdress. In some instances, a small child appears on the hip or at the breast. In others, a bulging abdomen suggests pregnancy.

The inspiration for these figures may have been awe and reverence for motherhood, fertility, and the continuity of life. Such sentiments would not have been unusual within early

■ A fertility figurine similar to those excavated in the Indus Valley. Such figurines are called "mother-goddesses." A typical Indus Valley goddess has an elaborate headdress and tubular limbs.

■ *Three views of a seal with the bull design. Thousands of such seals have been excavated. The majority of these seals depict bulls, powerful symbols of strength and virility.*

agricultural societies like that of the Indus Valley—the survival and well-being of these people depended on the bountiful gifts of nature. Therefore, early religious attention in the Indus Valley may have centered on fertility goddesses.

Other objects recovered from Harappa also support the idea that human sexual power and procreation were especially sacred to the people of the Indus Valley. Some, for example, depict bulls and various animals or female figures engaged in some sacred rite. The bull is believed to be a symbol of virility and sexual power. It is a motif commonly depicted in Indus Valley art; out of more than two thousand terra-cotta seals and seal impressions that have been found at the various archaeological sites, bulls predominate over other figures.

It seems that the Indus people considered the human figure to be inappropriate for expressing the sacredness of sexual power. Instead, animals, which were believed to have more strength and vitality than humans, were raised to a sacred status in Indus art works. The celebrations of their sexual fertility likewise stood for human sexuality.

Although not all the animals depicted on the seals were considered sacred, the importance of the bull continues in later Hindu mythology, where it is associated with an important Hindu god, *Shiva*. Shiva is a fertility god, the lord of beasts, who was sometimes depicted with three faces.

One of the most striking sacred seals of the Harappan culture depicts a horned god who strongly resembles Shiva. On the Harappan seals, this god is seated in a very formal posture—perhaps a posture of meditation—with the soles of his feet pressed together. His arms extend away from the body, his thumbs rest on his knees, and the other fingers point downward. He wears elaborate ornaments and a peculiar headdress consisting of a pair of buffalo horns with a plantlike object between them. Around him are four wild animals—an elephant, a tiger, a rhinoceros, and a buffalo—and beneath his stool are two deer. The surrounding animals and the plantlike growth on his head indicate that he is a fertility god. To the right and left of the head are small protuberances that are believed to represent second and third faces, like those of Shiva.

A man is shown traveling with his portable linga shrine. The abstract form of the male and female generative powers has been sacred from the time of the Indus Valley culture. Here, such an image, along with other religious paraphernalia, is being carried for the people on the roadside to worship.

From the artifacts of the Indus Valley, we gain some insight into the lifestyle and sacred beliefs that would begin to form the basis of Hinduism. We also know that the civilization of the Indus Valley was peaceful, and that it continued uninterrupted for more than one thousand years. This stability of Indus culture was due in part to the inner strength of its peoples and their ability to accept new ideas.

We do not know why the Indus civilization collapsed after such a long, peaceful, and comfortable period. As two possible causes, scholars look to climatic changes and the changing course of the Indus River and its tributaries. The coming of the Aryan invaders from the steppes of eastern Europe through Persia, could be another important cause.

The Invasion of the Aryans (Indo-Europeans)

The Aryans were one of the many Indo-European tribes that migrated outward from the steppes of eastern Europe. Some of the Aryan tribes journeyed across the mountains of Afghanistan into Pakistan and northwest India. There, more than four thousand years ago, they confronted the Indus Valley civilization.

The Aryans were seminomadic warriors who came to Pakistan and northwest India in two-wheeled, horse-drawn chariots. They brought a culture that sharply contrasted with that of the Indus people; the Aryans were skilled in bronze metalwork and had no interest in well-planned, fortified towns or agriculture or cattle raising. Although there is no evidence of Aryan architecture or of any art of quality and complexity, students of ancient civilization have excavated skillfully crafted metal weapons produced by this society.

Aryan literature was largely composed after the Aryans had settled in the Indus Valley. This literature clearly reflects the time when the Aryans confronted the Indus people. Some of their stories, for example, portray victories over a people called *dasas*—god-hating people addicted to strange religious rites.

The Aryans were patriarchal—they worshipped male gods. Goddess worship was unknown to them. Their major deities were gods who had links to the Sun, such as *Indra, Varuna,* and *Agni*. Aryan priests were poets who composed hymns in praise of their gods. Their hymns were intended to be sung during fire sacrifices made to appease the gods of the skies, the middle region, and the Earth.

By the time the Aryans arrived in the Indus Valley, the Indus culture in the valley was showing increasing signs of disorder. However, the Aryans did not enter a decayed cultural world. Many important religious elements, such as the reverence toward the Indus mother-goddess, control over sexual power, and ritual cleanliness, persisted in Indus village cultures.

At first, the Aryans ignored non-Aryan religious traditions. Later, however, they adopted some of the elements of Indus religions—those that their own religion could accommodate. Thus the Indus people and their beliefs gradually merged with the Aryan culture. The resulting culture was Aryan in structure, but it incorporated many local and non-Aryan beliefs and practices.

The Vedas and the Vedic Period

The Vedas were created by the Aryans who migrated toward northwest India from Persia. Like Hinduism itself, these holy scriptures have acquired many cultural and chronological layers. Some Vedic thoughts are so old that they reflect an Iranian origin that predates the migration of the Aryans to India in 1500 B.C.E. Other ideas in the Vedas evolved while Aryans lived in the Indus Valley. The content of these older texts was absorbed by the Aryans when they came to dominate the different cultures of the Indus Valley. There are four Vedas, the oldest and primary scriptures of Hinduism. The Vedas provide much historical, sociological, religious, and linguistic information about the people who composed them. They also provide a foundation for many Hindu religious concepts.

The word *veda* means "knowledge." The knowledge that the Vedas contain was considered to be of divine origin, revealed by the creator-god Brahman to a group of inspired sages. These sages, or *rishis,* were given the responsibility of transmitting the divine gift to humankind.

For centuries, the Vedas were passed by teachers to students through an oral tradition. Even when an alphabet was introduced, there was strong opposition to committing the Vedas to writing. The *Brahmins* (priests) believed that the power of the holy Vedic hymns lay in the tradition of hearing the text, thus the name for such hymns: *shruti,* or "that which is heard." Memorizing the Vedas from written words, according to the Brahmins, brought one no great religious strength. Eventually, however, for the sake of preservation, these holy hymns were written in an old form of Sanskrit that we now call *Vedic.*

In all, there are four Vedas. The Rig-Veda is by far the oldest collection of hymns. Although a precise date for its origin is impossible to pinpoint, scholars estimate the range from 5000 B.C.E. to 900 B.C.E. The present written text can be estimated to have existed by at least 300 B.C.E.

The Rig-Veda contains hymns and praises to the gods. The second Veda, composed around 700 B.C.E., is called the Yajur Veda. It contains a variation of the Rig-Veda text. In addition, it provides details for performing sacrifices, building altars, and reciting ritual phrases. In essence, it is the Brahmins' handbook.

The two remaining Vedas—Sama Veda and Atharva Veda—contain significant portions of the Rig-Veda, and both offer supplementary guidelines for priestly behavior. However, some differences do exist between these two Vedas. Parts of the Sama Veda, for example, center on sacrifices to *Soma*, a god of enthusiasm and intoxication whose worship developed from an undiscovered stimulant akin to the intoxication brought on by certain wild mushrooms. The hymns of the Atharva Veda are more concerned with magic spells, charms, and incantations. These fall into one of two categories: those of a healing, medicinal nature, such as love potions, cure-alls, and blessings; and those of a negative character, calling down misfortune or sickness upon enemies.

Early Vedic religion centered on divine power. The gods, called *devas*, comprised a pantheon (community) of divine powers. The number of the gods was not important—rather, the functions of the gods or the way they were associated with natural events or phenomena were important. Devas were classified as celestial, atmospheric, or terrestrial, depending on the primary location of their activity: sky, atmospheric region, and Earth.

Celestial Gods

The Vedic people believed in many celestial gods: Varuna, the guardian of cosmic law; *Mitra*, Varuna's chief assistant and a friend and benefactor of humankind; *Surya*, who represented the physical aspect of the Sun; and *Savitri*, who represented the Sun's ability to stimulate life.

To invite the celestial gods down to Earth, into their special places of prayer and worship, the early Hindus performed rituals. The god was honored with an offering of food and hymns of praise. A typical sacrificial hymn contained an invocation, or calling, to the god, offered in a tone of friendliness, reverence, or fear—depending on the god and one's relation to the god. The following is one such Vedic hymn, offered to the sky god Varuna:

> *Forgive, O gracious Lord, forgive! Whatever sin we*
> *mortals have committed against the people of the gods;*
> *if, foolish, we have thwarted your decrees, O god,*
> *do not destroy us in your anger!* (Basham 240)

Varuna was one of the most important gods of the early Vedic period. He was the overseer of moral action, and his guidance was the standard for cosmic, moral, and religious order.

This order is called *rita*. Varuna created the world and ruled it by the standard of rita. Rita also provided a structure for other celestial devas.

Vishnu was a minor celestial god during the early Vedic period. Later, Vishnu would become one of the three major gods of Hinduism. His main distinction in the Vedas was the three strides by which he crossed the Earth, the atmosphere, and then reached "the highest place," his special heaven. This ability was a significant factor in his later rise to prominence.

Atmospheric Gods

Hindus of the early Vedic period also believed in another class of devas. These were the atmospheric gods who included Indra, the god of lightning and thunder; *Vayu*, the god of wind; the *Maruts*, a troop of storm gods; and *Rudra*, the father of the Maruts.

Indra, a model warrior, was a figure of great popularity and prestige. In fact, he was the second most important god of the early Vedic era. The key to his character was a myth describing his conquest of the demon *Vritra*, a serpentine monster who blocked the flow of life-giving waters to the Aryans. It is said that Indra not only slew this mythic enemy; he also fought the real enemies of the Aryans, the *dasas*, or slaves, of the Indus Valley. Indra is called the Fortress Splitter and is praised for his destruction of the fortified citadels of Aryan opponents. With his belly full of exhilarating drink and his thunderbolt ready, Indra represented what an Aryan warrior aspired to be.

Rudra, the father of the Maruts, or storm gods, was feared because of his malevolent and destructive nature. He was also praised at times for his ability to protect his people from misfortune by sending storms upon their enemies. Rudra was a minor deva, far overshadowed by Varuna and Indra during this early Vedic period. In later Hinduism, however, his characteristics merged with the qualities of a non-Aryan, Indus Valley deity—an early form of the god Shiva. He then became one of the three major Hindu gods.

CHAPTER 3

The Late Vedic Period and the Upanishadic Period

*A*round the ninth century B.C.E., Aryan tribes migrated slowly across the plains of northern India to the Ganges Valley. By about the end of the seventh century B.C.E., Aryans as well as non-Aryans occupied the Ganges Valley. They were organized into distinct principalities, or states. Some were ruled by hereditary rulers called *rajahs*. Others, who were still in community groups of largely non-Aryan clans, were governed by chieftains. The principalities were populated by people of various ethnic compositions. There were light-skinned Aryans, dark-skinned Indus Valley people, and local tribal people of the Ganges Valley who had distinct skin coloration.

In the areas they occupied, the Aryans formed the upper strata of a still-fluid social order. Below them were the non-Aryans. This separation among the classes was not hard and fast. However, the Brahmins distinguished four classes of people: Brahmins, the priests; the ruling *Rajanyas* or *Kshatriyas* who, for the most part, were warriors; the *Vaishyas*, or common people such as artisans and farmers; and the *Shudras,* servants who are thought to have been non-Aryan natives.

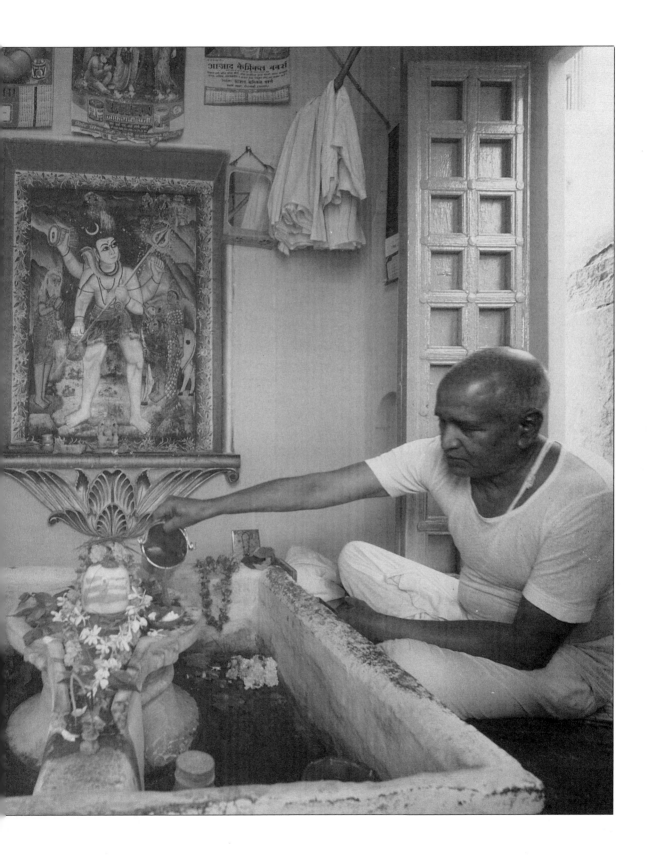

The belief in separate classes, the caste system, was supported and given religious sanction by a hymn in the Vedic scripture.

In the late Vedic period, the Aryans' worldview gradually changed. Major gods of the early Vedic period lost their importance. In later Vedic writings, interest shifted away from celestial and atmospheric gods toward devas who were located on the land. Also, more attention was directed toward sacrificial rituals.

It was during this period that the Brahmins, or priests, gained importance and power in early Hindu society. Eventually, people came to question the Brahmins' role. The period following the Vedic period, the already-mentioned era of the Upanishads, showed the results of this questioning.

Through the Upanishadic era, the religious history of the Hindus was never static. There had been a dynamic process of growth and innovation throughout the early period. From the hymns of the Vedas to the compilations of the Brahmanas and the Aranyakas (The forest books), there was a constant growth that followed the changing times of the society. The Upanishadic period likewise was vibrant with new ideas, speculation, and knowledge. The rejection of beliefs with which people could not identify and the quest for new answers filled the teachings of the Upanishads and inspired new schools of thought.

Terrestrial Gods and the Importance of Sacrifice

Sacrifice became an important part of Hindu life in the late Vedic period. As a result, only gods directly associated with sacrifices—such as Agni, the god of fire; Soma, the god of sacrificial libation or the pouring of drinks; and *Brahaspati,* the divine priest and lord of prayer—retained the interest of the later Vedic priests. In this later era, Varuna, Indra, and others only received minor sacrifices.

During this era, the religious life of the Hindus became increasingly dominated by the rituals performed around a fire pit. These so-called fire-sacrifice rituals gradually became very complex. Fire was now believed to be the creative source of all the powers of the gods and of nature. Fire rituals were of two kinds: *griha,* domestic rituals performed by the householder or priests, and *shrauta,* specialized rites performed by priests for patrons who paid for the sacrifice.

In *shrauta* rituals, Vedic hymns were recited by the Brahmin. The *shrauta* sacrifices were complicated, and over time, they became more and more elaborate and complex. Sacrificial duties, then, had to be divided among several priests. Performing the sacrifice, once meant to be a celebration of the devas, gradually came to be viewed as bringing power in its own right. Thus priests came to hold a lot of power in Hindu society.

While rites performed by priests became more complicated, *griha,* or domestic rites, remained simple. They celebrated the new and full moons, the seasons of the year, and the first fruit of the harvest, or they marked special family occasions such as the building of a new house, the birth of a son, and the passage through important stages of life. *Griha* rites could be performed on a household fire maintained by a pious parent, following the rituals spelled out over the years by the priests.

Gradually, the distinction between the *shrauta* and *griha* rituals became obscured, because both types of rites were subject to priestly influence and control. Even though *griha* rituals could be performed at home, they were still taught by priests and controlled

■ *Two priests performing the* **shrauta** *ritual using* **Agni**—*the god of fire*—*as the central element.*

by priests. Interestingly, most domestic rituals have been handed down from Vedic times to the present with little change or elaboration. Today, however, priests do not control the *griha* rituals.

During fire sacrifices, people offered their possessions to the gods. The most important sacrificial offerings were placed in a fire. People believed that the god Agni conveyed their offerings to the other gods through the fire. Agni was thought to be both the god of fire and the sacrificial fire itself. As the god of fire, he was the medium through which humans could relate to the other gods:

> *You, O Agni, are Indra, the bull of all that exists;*
> *You are the wide striding Vishnu, worthy of reverence;*
> *O Lord of the Holy Word (Brahaspati),*
> *you are the chief priest.*
>
> *. . . You, O Agni, are King Varuna, whose laws are firm;*
> *You are Mitra, the wonder-worker to be revered . . .*
> *You, O Agni, are Rudra, the Asura of lofty heaven;*
> *As the troops of Maruts, you control sustenance.*
> *(Rig-Veda II.1, 3, 4, 6 Hopkins 18)*

In sacrifices, Agni represented all the other gods. As the messenger to them, Agni linked humankind to the divine world. Because he could assume various forms of fire, Agni was believed to be an example of the divine world throughout nature.

Agni quickly became an all-important deity. In the celestial region, Agni was the Sun. In the atmospheric region, he was lightning. Finally, by lightning he was brought to the earth, and rekindled as fire from the trees in which he was hidden. When *shrauta* rituals were performed, three kinds of fire were kept so that they might symbolically represent Agni of the sky, of the atmosphere, and of the earth.

In the late Vedic period, other sacrificial elements also grew in importance. In particular, the element of sound and the sacred actions accompanying repetitive sound became essential to the sacrifice. During the offering of sacrifices, ritual statements called *mantras*, or verse prayers, were recited. Mantras were thought to capture the power of Brahman, the Upanishadic Ultimate Reality. Because of their deep wisdom, and often because of their

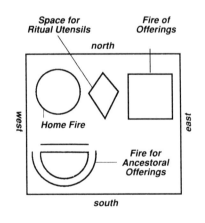

■ Diagram of a sacrificial plot used for the **shrauta** ritual.

magical power, the mantras or the sacred speech soon became more important to know than the natural world. Eventually, sacred speech was deified in the form of the goddess *Vac* (meaning "speech").

The gods themselves are said to have performed sacrifices to obtain their places in the Vedic heaven. Although the early Vedas are not known for stories of creation, by the end of the oldest and most important Veda, the Rig-Veda, such a story had developed. The story told of a god known as *Prajapati*, the lord of beings, who was also known as *Purusha*. It was believed that he existed before the foundation of the universe. Prajapati was a primeval human being who was sacrificed by the gods, who were his children. From the body of this divine victim, the universe was created. The "Hymn of the Primeval Man," from the Rig-Veda, describes this first cosmic sacrifice that brought forth the universe:

When the gods made a sacrifice with the Man (Purusha) as their victim, Spring was the melted butter, Summer the fuel, and Autumn the oblation. From that all-embracing sacrifice the clotted butter was collected. From it he made the animal of air and wood and village. From that all-embracing sacrifice were born the hymns and chants, from that the meters were born, from that the sacrificial spells were born. Thence were born horses, and all beings with two rows of teeth. Thence were born cattle, and thence goats and sheep. When they divided the Man, into how many parts did they divide him? What was his mouth, what were his arms, what were his thighs and his feet called? The Brahmin was his mouth, of his arms was made the Kshatriya, his thighs became the Vaishya, of his feet the Shudra was born. The moon arose from his mind. From his eye was born the sun. From his mouth Indra and Agni. From his breath the wind was born. From his navel came the air. From his head there came the sky, from his feet the earth, the four quarters from his ear. Thus they fashioned the world. With Sacrifice the gods sacrificed to sacrifice.

These were the first of the sacred laws. The mighty
beings reached the sky, where are the eternal spirits, the
gods. (Basham 242–243)

In this poem, parallels are made between Purusha's sacrificed body and all the levels of creation. All creation is given a religious association in which Purusha, the cosmic victim, is centrally important. The cosmos, the world of nature, human society, and sacrifice are seen as similar and parallel, all created at the same time for all ages by Purusha's sacrifice.

According to the poem, the sacrifice of Purusha, the cosmic victim, is the reference point for all things. His sacrifice is the key to creation. Early Hindus believed that all other sacrifices were imitations of this great sacrifice. Furthermore, they also believed that to know Purusha's sacrifice was to know the universe.

Brahmins and Power

Throughout much of the Vedic period, the Brahmins (priests) held a central place of power in society. This was in part because the Brahmins controlled and oversaw the sacrifices in which the gods came down to Earth to partake in offerings by their devotees. As mentioned, these included *shrauta* and *griha* rituals. The Brahmins also held additional power because they controlled knowledge of the Vedas.

The Vedas were passed from teacher to student in the oral tradition. They had to be studied and memorized by priests and then told to members of other castes. Because of this, members of the priestly caste could literally hold the knowledge within their caste. Brahmins not only knew the sacrificial hymns and prayers by heart, but they were considered to be the only specialists qualified to perform the holy fire sacrifices for the people. Thus the Brahmins controlled common access to the gods and ultimately to the entire cosmos.

By the end of the Vedic period, the Brahmins had made a supplementary addition to each of the four Vedas. These four compilations were called Brahmanas. They contained guidance for priests in the use of hymns and prayers. The Brahmanas gave practical directions, in exhaustive detail, for carrying out all types of sacrifice.

To explain the deeper meaning of these complex rites, still more explanations had to be compiled. These further explanations were known as Aranyakas, or forest books, because the teaching of them took place in forest retreats. Although the Brahmanas insisted on proper ritual actions, the Aranyakas seemed to claim that the understanding of the meaning behind the ritual actions was more important. They claimed that perfect ritual did not depend on elaborate fire sacrifices but could be performed within one's own mind. The compilation of the Brahmanas and Aranyakas clearly shows how fascinated and absorbed the Vedic priests were with their rituals and the process of elaborating on them and interpreting them.

The use of the Brahmanas' rituals was limited to those who were considered to be ritually pure and fit. A knowledge of the proper ritual actions brought people offering sacrifices into the company of those having direct access to the gods. If the rituals were properly performed by the priests throughout their lives, it was believed that after death, both the priests and those who asked them to offer the sacrifices would be rewarded with an existence freed from their mortal bodies. In short, they would be elevated to the world of the gods.

Over time, many people became disenchanted with the complex rituals mandated by the Brahmins. Also, the idea that the universe was formed and maintained through Purusha's sacrifice lost religious support. Different ideas about the world's creation and life's meaning gained attention.

One widely believed theory stated that the world could be explained in terms of a neutral, or impersonal, principle. This principle was known simply as "that One." The following hymn contains an alternative explanation for the creation of the universe. It clearly questions the early Vedic vision of creation:

Then there were neither death nor immortality,
Nor was there then the torch of night and day.
That One breathed windlessly and self-sustaining;
There was that One then, and there was no other.
At first there was only darkness wrapped in darkness;
All this was only unillumined water.
That one which came to be, enclosed in nothing,

Arose at last, born of the power of heat (tapas).
In the beginning desire (Kama, creative or
sacrificial impulse) descended on it—
that was the primal seed, born of the mind . . .
But, after all, who knows, and who can say
Whence it all came, and how creation happened?
The gods themselves are later than creation,
So who knows truly whence it has arisen?
Whence all creation had its origin?
He, whether he fashioned it or whether he did not,
He, who surveys it all from highest heaven,
He knows, or perchance he knows not.
(Rig-Veda X.129.6, 7)

As a result of spiritual and social questioning, a way of life quite in contrast to all the complex rituals of the Brahmins became increasingly common at this time. This was the lifestyle of people known as *ascetics*. Ascetics are dedicated to great austerity and self-discipline in their lives. In late Vedic times, they tended to live as hermits in the forest and chose not to participate in the Hindu social structure with its many castes.

Ascetics emerged from all sections of society and rivaled the Brahmins, or priests, in commanding the highest respect of the people. The passion that fueled the austere devotion of the ascetic in the forest was itself revered as sacrificial; this passionate dedication to the austere life was compared to a fire on the altar. The repetition of Vedic chants that characterized the lives of the Vedic priests was thought to be equivalent to the austere devotion of these ascetics. The heat of such ascetic devotion and prayer was called *tapas,* or the heat of knowledge. The simple and sincere acts of the ascetics were thought to bring a higher understanding of the Ultimate Reality. Indeed, it allowed the ascetics to have a higher understanding of all reality.

The ascetics, or forest hermits, were also adept in various forms of meditation, or quiet thinking. Some were called *munis* (silent ones) and others, *rishis* (having the power of knowledge). The *munis* were described as those who ". . . wear the wind as a girdle, and who are drunk with their own silence. They know the thoughts of all the people, for they have drunk the magic cup of Rudra/Shiva, which is poison to ordinary mortals."

Because ascetics led lives of austerity and purity, it was believed that they could generate "the heat of deep knowledge" by their acts of meditation and by their ascetic practices. People began to believe more and more that without priests, they themselves could experience the power of meditation and ascetic practice to bring on deep religious knowledge. Meditation and asceticism were seen as keys to religious fervor, and they were available to forest hermits as well as to those who wanted to imitate their activities.

The religious example of the ascetics presented an alternative religious form of life for many people. The Vedic tradition of the Brahmins seemed centered on the priests and the exact performance of their rituals. Having become, to some degree, disenchanted with the elaborate sacrifices of the Brahmins, many people wanted to know if there was some higher goal to life than offering exactly performed sacrifices. People began to search for a state of immortality, a life not ruled by death and not eroded by time. They also wondered how such a state could be obtained—how they might transcend or overcome the defeating condition of a life where there seemed to be no hope of something greater. Hindus of the Upanishadic period tried to answer some of these new religious questions.

The Upanishadic Period

The Upanishadic period (800–450 B.C.E.) was one of the greatest eras of creative thinking in the history of Hinduism. During this period, people took a more questioning attitude toward human existence. Upanishadic ascetics were philosophers, teachers, and seers. They lived in forest hermitages. They spent their days studying, contemplating, and discussing the puzzling questions of the universe. Young minds were attracted to these hermitages, hoping to engage in debates there and thus find enlightenment.

The Upanishads were composed by these forest hermits around 700–500 B.C.E., as the last section of the Vedas. They are also known as *shruti*, or "listened to" texts, and almost all of their

An **Upanishadic** sage/philosopher in a forest hermitage discusses the meaning of life and the nature of reality with his student.

teachings are in the form of dialogues. The meaning of the word *Upanishad* is "sitting down near" a guru (spiritual master) who passes on his secret teachings. More than 100 compilations of these dialogues are written down, though only 13 of them are accepted as *smriti*, or sacred scriptures. Generally, the Upanishads discuss the relationship between the individual and the universe, the nature of the universal soul, the meaning of life, and the character of life after death.

The Upanishadic period introduced to Hinduism a new and influential kind of thinking and questioning. In principle, these texts differed from the Vedas in that they did not exclude people outside the Brahmin caste. However, the content of the Upanishads is subtle and profound. Since understanding the Upanishadic concepts has been considered a difficult task, only a few, in fact, come to a deep knowledge of their teachings.

Despite the complexity of the Upanishads, men and women of all classes participated in Upanishadic learning. It was not one's class or caste but one's character that was important. Honesty, for example, was much more highly valued in a potential student at a hermitage than was a person's family tree. One passage from the Upanishads poignantly expresses how much the inner person was appreciated within this religious community:

Satyakama was the son of a woman named Jabala. One day her son asked, "Mother, I want to be a student. What is my family name?" His mother replied, "My dear, I don't know your family. I had you when I was very young traveling as a servant. My name is Jabala, and yours is Satyakama, so you are Satyakama Jabala." The next day the boy went to a teacher by the name of Gautama Haridrumata, and said: "I want to be your student, sir. Can I?" The teacher asked what his family name was. Satyakama replied, "I don't know my family, sir. I asked my mother and she said that she had me in her youth, when she traveled about a lot as a servant . . . She said she was Jabala and I was Satyakama and that I was to give my name as Satyakama Jabala." The teacher replied, "Nobody but a true brahman would be so honest!" He said, "Go and fetch me fuel, my friend, and I will initiate you, for you have not swerved from the truth."

Two of the oldest (circa 700–500 B.C.E.) and most significant of the Upanishadic scriptures are the Brihadaranyaka Upanishad and the Chandogya Upanishad. In the Chandogya Upanishad, a question is posed so that its answer can show the relationship between the sacrificial fire on the altar, the fire in the Sun, and tapas (the heat of understanding). The question is about the creative powers in the universe. It is formulated in this way: What is the nature of the One that is the cause of the whole of existence? The answer discusses the creative powers of tapas, of sacrifice, and of the ultimate truth, Brahman.

Students of the Upanishads believed that it was not the ritual acts of sacrifices themselves, but rather the spirit behind the sacrifices that was important. They believed that through meditation or reflection they could attain the knowledge of how they were related to the gods and how this divine link originated. They also wanted to know what were their real selves and what was the relationship of their real selves to the Universal Reality, that is, Brahman.

Such spiritual reflection and searching was believed to cause *tapas* within the dedicated student. By setting aside all other concerns, the student really was "sacrificing" them. In this respect, these individuals set aside or "sacrificed" worldly concerns and thereby performed sacrifices on the altar of their hearts. Such self-sacrifices paralleled the fire sacrifices of the Vedic priests.

Upanishadic ascetics sacrificed their selves, disciplined their bodily concerns, and desired enlightenment. They believed that this showed a power to transcend worldly cares and contemplate the important questions of reality. Such practices led to a belief that an individual had, beyond a surface self, an essential or real self. The question, then, was to ask what this essential self was and how one could grasp it. This question, which is still important in modern Hinduism, was answered in part by a new idea of the Ultimate.

In the Upanishads, all the many gods of the Vedic tradition are reduced to one, Brahman. Brahman was believed to be the supreme essence of the universe. This essence is seen in the universe, in the various creations of the physical world, and in the soul of individuals.

A major focus of the Upanishadic thinkers was the idea that an individual's soul, called atman, was a separated part of Brahman, or the universal soul. Since the Upanishadic era, Hindus have believed that atman, the individual soul, is Brahman, the universal soul. It has been separated as atman but after achieving *moksha*, or salvation, it will be united again with Brahman. Eventually, the word *Brahman* was used to refer to the universal essence containing all kinds of power.

The idea of atman-Brahman is repeated in the famous phrase from the Chandogya Upanishad, "*tat tvam asi*," literally, "that thou art." This phrase means that there is no difference between the individual and the universal. A story from the Chandogya Upanishad well illustrates this connection:

Svetaketu asked his father-teacher to make him understand what Atman and Brahman were. Father said,

"Fetch me a fruit of the banyan tree." "Here is one, sir." "What do you see?" "Very tiny seeds, sir." "Break one." "I have broken it, sir." "Now what so you see?" "Nothing, sir." "My son," the father said, "what you do not perceive is the essence, and in that essence the mighty banyan tree exists. Believe me, my son, in that essence is the Self of all that is. That is the True, that is the Self. Tat tvam asi. And you are that Self, Svetaketu."

In this story, the soul is depicted as the innermost or the real self. This innermost self is in no sense a physical thing. The identity of the soul of the individual and the soul of the universe is the central theme throughout the Upanishadic texts. *Tat tvam asi*, "you [the individual soul] are that [the universal essence]" is the principal teaching of the period. Another story illustrating this truth is found in the Brihadaranyaka Upanishad:

"Put this salt in water, and come to me in the morning." The student did as he was told. In the morning the teacher said, "Fetch the salt." The student looked for it, but could not find it, because it had dissolved. "Taste the water from the top, said the teacher. "How does it taste?" "Of salt," the student replied. "Taste from the middle. How does it taste?" "Of salt," the student replied. "Taste from the bottom. How does it taste?" "Of salt," the student answered. Then the teacher said, "You don't perceive that one Reality exists in your own body, my dear, but it is truly there. Everything which has its being is that subtle essence. That is Reality! That is the Soul! And you are that, Svetaketu!"

Samsara, Karma, and *Moksha*

Of the many Upanishadic teachings that were to become permanent elements of Hinduism, those of samsara and karma are the most prominent. By the time of the Upanishads, many Hindus considered that the everyday world, brought forth and maintained by gods, might be a trap in which people could be caught up in continuing cycles of birth, death, and rebirth.

Conceivably, this could go on forever. The concept of samsara gave some hope that one might improve one's condition.

Samsara is a belief in the transmigration, or continual passing, of a soul from one body to another. It can be described as follows. The soul of a person who dies does not pass into heaven, or hell, or elsewhere. It is reborn into another body, which may be of a higher or lower order than one's previous existence. Rebirth follows rebirth in an endless chain. Thus, a person of low status may be reborn as a priest, or a king, or an animal, or even a worm. The question then arises: What causes the soul to enter a higher or lower state of existence?

A person's higher or lower state of existence is determined by the law of karma (the law of deeds or works.) This is a law determining that an individual's thoughts, words, and deeds have ethical consequences that establish the quality of the person's future existences. For Hindus, the law of karma is a necessary law of nature. It decides the quality of a Hindu's further life. A person who has done good deeds is reborn into a good existence in the next birth, and if he or she has done bad deeds, had evil thoughts, and spoken bad words, the person is reborn as an animal.

Karma does not only apply to one's future life; it also applies to what happens in one's present life. According to the law of karma, the good that a person does in this life eventually comes back to him or her in the form of good fortune, either in one's present life or in one's future existence. Likewise, a person pays a "karmic price" for the evil deeds he or she might have performed. The evil deed will come back to "haunt" the person in this present life or in a future existence.

The highest of the Upanishadic teachings completes the ideas of samsara and karma. This is the concept of *moksha*, or release: by leading a good spiritual life, that is, by union with Brahman, or the Ultimate Reality, an individual will eventually leave the temporary existences and the cycle of samsara. With the idea of *moksha*, the desire for eternal oneness with Brahman became more important than improving one's position in this life or gaining physical enjoyment by good deeds or karma.

In the Upanishadic era, Hindus gradually placed an increasingly higher value on the goal of union with the Universal Soul

■ A **yogi** can be recognized by his matted, tangled hair. He has no possessions. He wears a loose cloak and carries with him a wooden staff and a flute. He has renounced his social status in order to find the highest truth (**Brahman**) through mental and physical discipline. His goal is to be spiritually united with **Brahman** in order to achieve salvation, **moksha.**

and release from the realm of samsara. *Moksha* came to be considered the highest and perhaps the sole purpose of life. Over the years, various Hindu sects strove toward this same goal, but they did so through different methods.

Along with the new ideas of sacrifice, god, and the cycle of samsara, the Upanishadic period also saw many new schools of religious philosophy. One of these was yoga. Yoga is a form of physical and mental discipline. Although its practice was much older than the Upanishads, the common methods of yoga were further developed and explained in this era. Upanishadic seers followed yogic techniques that emphasized the difference between the body and the self.

Those who practiced yoga believed that it could lead them to a state in which atman became one with Brahman. This was possible because the self in its deepest reality was believed already to be like Brahman—pure, limitless, and unchanging. People who practiced yoga and had this special experience of union with Brahman were called *jivanmukta* (those who are liberated while still alive).

Vedanta was another powerful school of religious philosophy that emerged at this time. It fostered the idea that there was an underlying unity to all reality. It introduced the concept of *maya*, an impersonal force that makes people forget that all individuals are part of the universal essence. Maya is believed to be the cause of all ignorance and suffering and must be overcome.

New Methods of Teaching

The instruction of the Upanishads promised a religious teaching that would be centered on ordinary people and not on the detailed sacrificial rites of the Brahmins. However, many common people had difficulty understanding the texts. The Upanishadic teachings were simply too philosophical and puzzling. During the same time as the Upanishadic period, some non-Brahmin thinkers, such as Buddhists and Jains, came to reject the old sacrificial tradition of the Brahmins. These teachers began to convey their religious lessons in new ways—through the telling of stories and parables.

Coming out of the confines of the forest schools that had been the classrooms of the Upanishads, the new teachers traveled from one town to the next. While traveling, they told stories and spread their beliefs and ideas. The people listened eagerly and were entranced by the simple parables. They found the teachings uplifting. They also discovered that the stories brought them understanding of their lives and of the world.

Soon the stories and parables, which often illustrated moral or religious lessons, became very popular. Seeing that this approach to religious teaching was successful, even the Brahmins began to adopt storytelling as part of their preaching method. Consequently, new forms of Brahmanic literature came into existence around the third century B.C.E. At that time, the Brahmins wrote new literature as well as additions to older works. Some examples of how the Brahmins adapted the new teaching methods can be seen in the additions they made to the great epic poems, the *Ramayana* and the *Mahabharata,* and also to the sacred writings known as the *Puranas.*

Originally, the *Ramayana* and the *Mahabharata* were long, nonreligious stories about the exploits and struggles of warriors and kings, told by generations of traveling bards. Later, all sorts of material was added to these basic stories. So much material was incorporated into the original stories that each of the great epics, especially the *Mahabharata,* developed into an encyclopedia of heroes and legends—some legends giving historical portraits, some creating mythological images. It is in the epics that one encounters the ever-developing characters of the great gods Shiva and Vishnu, their wives, their families, and numerous other minor gods.

Whereas the epics seem to have reached their final form by 500 C.E., the *Puranas* continued to develop until late in the 12th century C.E. The *Puranas,* or "old stories," incorporate legends, myths, and customary observances. Later portions of the *Puranas* focused on stories of the gods *Brahma,* Vishnu, and Shiva. Hindus worshipped each of these three gods separately, but the three were also considered to be one god with three functions: creation (Brahma), preservation (Vishnu), and destruction (Shiva).

The myths and legends of the *Puranas* brought meaning to people's lives. Because the legends were often intertwined with significant historical facts, the *Puranas* were often associated with *itihasa* (history). Like the epics, Puranic texts are considered important because they have been, and still are, the media of mass education in the Hindu world. For centuries, religious, social, and cultural norms and inspirations have been imparted through this type of literature.

While many works may bear the name *purana,* only 18 are traditionally acknowledged as *shruti,* or sacred. These are called the *Mahapuranas,* "great old stories." It is also true that any religious text could be called a minor purana. Many minor puranas that were written after the older *shruti* were referred to as *mahatmyas,* or "glorifications." These mostly glorified gods and places of pilgrimage. Among these are modern *Mahatmyas,* some composed as recently as the 19th century.

CHAPTER 4

The Gods and Religious Devotion

During the period between 500 B.C.E. and 400 C.E., the *Puranas* were inspired by various Hindu sects. Within each sect, individuals considered one god to be their personal god and the highest god. What developed with this more personal religious perspective was a popular devotional movement known as *bhakti*, "attachment," or fervent devotion to a god.

The seeds of this new approach to religion had been sown in the earlier traditions of both the epics and the *Puranas*. We can see how the seeds developed if we study some of the stories of the gods and the people's new appreciation of certain gods. In the earlier periods, these gods had small roles within the Hindu pantheon. They took on new dimensions and gained in importance as the years moved on.

The Ambiguous God Shiva

Shiva was not a prominent god in the earlier writings of the Brahmins. In the Vedas, the forerunner of the god Shiva was the terrible atmospheric deva Rudra, an Aryan god of storms, lightning, and medicinal herbs. Because Rudra controlled

■ Preceding page—
Rama, Sita, and
Lakshamana on their
way to the forest after
being banished by
Rama's stepmother. In
this picturesque land-
scape, they are being
served by the forest
hermits.

atmospheric forces, the Indus Valley people believed that he could direct human destiny. In return for the prayers of his worshippers, Rudra gave them healing remedies and protected them against the destruction brought by powerful storms.

By the period of the Upanishads, Rudra's characteristics merged with those of another Indus Valley terrestrial god of cattle to form Shiva, one of three major gods. He was the Indus yogic god having control over sexuality. He was the Vedic god of terrible rains and storms and the healing god of herbs. In addition, he was the deity of animals, the father of storm gods, and the god

■ Shiva is shown here
with his wife Parvati and
their two sons Skanda
and Ganesha. This
picture depicts both
the benign and the ter-
rible symbols of Shiva.
Although the holy family
is seated in the middle
of a calm and peaceful
landscape, the fore-
ground shows a crema-
tion ground with burning
pyres and bones from
human skeletons.

of yogic power. He became known for his contradictory powers, particularly sexual power and the power of yogic self-control. Religious awe of the complex figure of Shiva and his wife, *Parvati,* merged into the tradition of Shiva worship—referred to as Shaivism—during the early decades (third century B.C.E.) of the Puranic time period.

Many myths provide absorbing portraits of Shiva's multi-sided nature. These myths occur often in the epics and the *Puranas.* Each time, the stories are told a bit differently, depending on the storyteller and the time they were written down.

One myth about Shiva tells how the gods were constantly struggling with demons (*raksasas*). To strengthen themselves in their struggle, the gods decided to use *amrita,* the elixir of immortality. To produce this elixir, they had to churn the Ocean of Milk. The gods used the serpent Vasuki as their churning rope. Having been churned around for some time, the serpent vomited forth poison. Just as the poison was about to fall into the elixir, contaminate it, and destroy all hope for the gods, Shiva, the god of gods, came to the rescue. He caught the poison in his mouth and saved the gods' drink of immortality. He himself was saved from swallowing it by his wife, Parvati, who strangled him so that the poison would stay in his throat. This is why some portraits of Shiva give him a blue throat.

In the *Mahabharata,* Shiva is worshipped not only as creator of the universe but also as the primeval father. The great epic tells of Shiva living in the Himalayas with his wife, Parvati (a beneficent and mild form of the great goddess *Mahadevi Shakti*), and their two sons, *Ganesha* and *Skanda.* They also live with Shiva's constant companion and *vahana* (vehicle), Nandi, the bull—a symbol of male strength and power.

Throughout the Hindu legends, Shiva is depicted in many different forms. A popular form of Shiva is that of the lord of dance, *Nataraja.* His sacred cosmic dance has the power to remove all evils and obstacles. Nataraja stands in a posture of dance in the middle of a fiery halo. This flaming *mandorla* represents the universe with all its illusion, suffering, and pain.

Within this universe, Nataraja dances. The locks of his hair are decked with a crescent moon, a skull, and a tiny symbol of the sacred river Ganges. The skull, with its faint smile, laughs at people who consider themselves eternal, unable to realize how fleeting life is. The crescent moon in his matted hair keeps *Kama,* the god of nightly love, alive, and through the waxing and waning of the moon he creates different seasons and rejuvenates life. The river Ganges that flows in Nataraja's hair originally flowed in heaven. When the heavenly Ganges was needed on Earth, she was unwilling to descend because she realized that her fall from heaven would be too heavy for the Earth to withstand. So Shiva, as Nataraja, agreed to break the violent power of the sacred river's fall by catching her in his tangled hair.

Shiva also wears snakes coiled around his upper arms and his neck, symbolizing his control over these most deadly animals. Although snakes are the most dreaded poisonous animals on land, Shiva's power diminishes their terrible nature. Snakes also symbolize the transmigration or change that souls undergo as they inhabit different bodies. Snakes shed their skin in due season and grow a new one—just as in Hindu belief humans obtain a new body with each rebirth of their soul.

In two of his four hands, Shiva often holds a drum and a flame. The drum represents the rhythmic sound to which Nataraja dances and ceaselessly recreates the universe. The flames represent the destructive energy with which Nataraja dances at the end of each cosmic age, cleansing sins and removing illusion. His right hand blesses devotees. His left hand, pointing toward his foot, grants eternal bliss to those who approach him. The other foot treads firmly upon the dwarf of ignorance, allowing the birth of knowledge.

In addition, Shiva's form as Nataraja reveals a tradition that revered the power of female and male sexuality. From his left earlobe hangs a female earring and from his right earlobe a male earring. These symbolize the union of the archetypal parents of the universe.

The worship of sexual power that was prominent in pre-Aryan times had no place in the early Vedic hymns. However, the tradition of reverence for sexual power and the need for self-control was probably carried on for centuries outside the Vedas in the Brahmanic tradition. With the emergence in the Puranic

■ *The "auspicious" head of Shiva shows a crescent moon, indicating the phases of lunar time. A miniature form of the sacred river Ganges adorns Shiva's matted hair. A smiling skull adorns the front of his headgear, and his dissimilar earrings represent his male and female aspects.*

texts of both Shiva and *Shakti*—the primeval father and mother—the worship of sexual power resurfaced. And some of the most potent symbols in Hinduism are associated with Shiva as the god of regeneration and sexuality.

In Shaivism, which is the cult of Shiva worship, the central objects of worship are symbols of sexual power. Even the Ultimate Reality of Brahman is often represented by symbolic forms of the genitals, such as the pillar of light and the golden egg. At times, Mother Earth is referred to as the womb and Father Sky and Space as the *linga*, a symbol of male sexuality. In Puranic sacrificial rituals, the fire is called a linga, and the *yoni*, or hearth, is a symbol of female sexuality. Both are common Saivite symbols. The most commonly known linga is the fire linga, which is referred to as *Jyotirlinga*. In Hindu mythology, Jyotirlinga is one of the forms of the god Shiva.

In one myth, Shiva, as Jyotirlinga, asserts his supremacy over two other high gods, Brahma and Vishnu. The myth is told as follows:

One day, Brahma noticed Vishnu, with his thousand omniscient eyes, lying on the formless waters, supported by the thousand-headed serpent of the Infinite. Impressed by Vishnu's radiance, Brahma asked the eternal being who he was. Vishnu raised his sleepy lotus eyes, smiled, and beckoned to Brahma in a condescending manner. Brahma was offended by Vishnu's informal attitude, and responded, "How can you treat me as a master would his pupil? I am the cause of creation and destruction, the creator of a thousand universes, the source of all that exists!" Vishnu replied, "Don't you know that I am Narayana, creator, preserver, and destroyer of the worlds, eternal male, immortal source of the universe, and its center as well? Even thou are born of my indestructible body."

■ These three drawings depict three hand gestures of Shiva. In his upper right hand, he carries the drum, whose sound symbolizes the creation of the cosmos. In his upper left hand, he carries the flame, which symbolizes the simultaneous destruction of the cosmos. Shiva's lower hands are together in a gesture of blessing and reassurance.

Brahma and Vishnu thus argued bitterly above the formless sea, when a glorious, shimmering linga appeared before their eyes. The linga was a flamboyant pillar with the brilliance of a hundred fires, capable of consuming the universe. It was without beginning, without middle, and without end, incomparable and indescribable. Then the divine Vishnu, troubled as Brahma was by the flames, said to him, "We must look for the source of this fire. I shall go down in the form of a boar. You shall rise up in your manifestation of a swan."

Taking the shape of a blue boar with sharp tusks, a long snout, and firm, short feet, Vishnu plunged into the depths for a thousand years. However, despite his enduring effort, he could not find the base of the fire linga. Meanwhile, the white swan, with burning eyes and great wings, whose flight was as swift as the wind, soared for a thousand years to find the top of the pillar. He, too, was unable to reach it. Brahma was returning when he met the great Vishnu, likewise returning, weary and disconcerted. Suddenly they saw Shiva standing before them as Jyotirlinga. They bowed before him. Vishnu said to Shiva, "Our dispute has been blessed by you, the god of gods, since you appeared before us to put an end to our argument." Shiva replied, "I am supreme lord, undivided. I am three: Brahma, Vishnu and Shiva. I create, I maintain, I destroy."

Stories such as this one show Shiva's supremacy over all the other gods. Hindus have looked up to such sacred stories for examples of godlike behavior. They also gain insight into who and what it is they worship.

Sons of Shiva and Parvati

As Hindu mythology relates, Shiva and Parvati reside in the Himalayas with their sons, Ganesha and Skanda (who sometimes is called *Kartikeya*). Ganesha is an elephant-headed god, the remover of obstacles, who is invoked at the beginning of every Hindu undertaking. Skanda is an immortal warrior, the defender of the gods, who is associated with Agni and Indra.

Many different myths exist concerning the origin of Ganesha's elephant head. According to one account, Parvati, before starting to bathe one day, scraped the ointment from her body and mixed it with oils and other ointments. From this she formed a man's figure and gave it life by sprinkling it with water from the Ganges River. She then set this figure, her son Ganesha, outside the bathhouse door to stand guard. When Shiva tried

■ *This drawing depicts Shiva as the greatest of the three major Hindu gods. He appears as the linga of fire and is worshipped by the other two great gods, Brahma and Vishnu.*

to enter, Ganesha refused to let him in. As Shiva did not know him, he became angry and cut off Ganesha's head. When Parvati emerged and found her son dead, she was overwrought with grief. Shiva felt sympathy for his wife, so he sent a messenger to seek another head for the child. The first creature the messenger found was an elephant. He brought back the elephant's head, and this was planted on Ganesha's shoulders.

Other versions of Ganesha's origin suggest that Shiva created him in response to a request by the gods and sages, who had realized that there was no overseer of good or bad deeds. Shiva pondered over this lack of a guide for some time, then turned toward Parvati. As he looked at her, a radiant youth of great beauty, endowed with the qualities of Shiva, sprang forth from his gaze. All the heavenly hosts were amazed and captivated by his beauty.

Parvati was jealous and angered by her husband's production of such a beautiful son. She cursed the son, wishing that he would become ugly and have an elephant's head. Shiva countered her curse by declaring that despite his son's elephantine head, he would be the guardian of successes and failures and would rule over all occasions. He declared that Ganesha would be great among gods, that he would be the god of wisdom and prudence, that he would be a scribe and learned in all the scriptures. Today, Ganesha is represented as a short, pot-bellied man with four arms and an elephant head.

The stories of Ganesha that have been handed down over the many centuries show the complexity of his personality. These stories point to the variety of traditions that have gone to create the complex portraits we have of Ganesha. They also show how Hinduism has been a fluid religion, even in its portraits of the ever-surviving characters that descend from Shiva.

One story of Ganesha and his brother, Kartikeya, tells how they were rivals for the same wives. To settle their dispute, they agreed that whoever first circled the world would win the wife of his choosing. Kartikeya set off and after a long, wearying excursion, he returned home. There he found Ganesha—who had never left—already married to both young women. The elephant-headed brother explained to Kartikeya that instead of making the painstaking journey around the world, he had simply circled around their father, Shiva, who is the equivalent of the universe!

In some myths, Kartikeya is married to *Kumari*. In many others, he is portrayed as someone not interested in women. He rides a peacock, carries bows and arrows, and has six heads and six pairs of arms. Accounts of Kartikeya's origin and his strange appearance vary. In one very popular myth, the demon *Taraka* was creating havoc in the heavens, and the gods discussed how they could put an end to this tyranny. They decided that they had to persuade Shiva to have a son who would kill Taraka.

Unfortunately, Shiva was engaged most deeply in meditation. At the same time, Parvati was also deeply absorbed in meditation. Shiva took no notice of her, nor she of him. Seeing this, the gods ordered Kama, the god of love, to approach Shiva, the great ascetic, and stir up a strong desire in his heart for Parvati. Kama obediently went to Mount Kailasha in the Himalayas, saw Shiva meditating, and found beautiful Parvati gathering flowers. Kama thought Shiva could be attracted by Parvati's beauty, so he drew his arrow and let it fly. As the arrow struck Shiva, desire awoke in his heart. But then Shiva not only saw Parvati—he also saw Kama. He realized that the god of love was trying to manipulate him. This made Shiva so angry that he burned Kama to ashes instantly.

Though desire had been aroused in his heart, Shiva, the lord of asceticism, did not give way to his passion. He consented to marry Parvati, but no children were born. Again, the gods decided to take matters into their own hands. They sent Agni as their ambassador to urge Shiva to beget a son. Agni, disguised as a bird, flew around, watching Shiva constantly. Finally, he managed to pick up a seed of the great god in his beak. As he flew, his burden seemed to grow heavier and heavier until finally, as he was passing over the river Ganges, he was forced to drop it. There, on the banks of the Ganges, arose a child as beautiful as the moon and as brilliant as the sun. This was Kartikeya. As he appeared on the bank of the Ganges, six royal women came to bathe. Each of them wanted this beautiful son as her own and wished to feed him. So the newborn god acquired six mouths and was suckled by all of his foster mothers.

Vishnu and the Ten Avatars

In the period of the Vedas, Vishnu was a minor divinity. He was associated with the Aryan warrior god, Indra. Gradually, Vishnu gained importance, and by the time of the great epics he was a paramount deva of the Hindu trinity: Brahma, Shiva, and Vishnu.

Vishnu is known as a powerful but kind god. He is a father-like figure and a just ruler. He is worshipped with great devotion, and little fear. The Vaishnavites (the followers of Vishnu) worship Vishnu as the greatest of the gods, the preserver, and the ever-present spirit.

Vishnu is most commonly depicted as a handsome young man dressed in royal robes, reclining with his wife, *Lakshami,* on the coil of the serpent *Ananta* (or *Shesha*). He has four hands with which he holds a conch shell, a discus, a club, and a lotus flower. The *Garuda,* a creature half man and half eagle, is Vishnu's *vahana* (vehicle). Vishnu resides in a heavenly city called Vaikuntha, which is said to be made entirely of gold and precious jewels. This city is located on the mythical Mount Meru. The river Ganges, which according to some myths has its source in Vishnu's foot, flows through the city. In the pools of this heaven grow blue, red, and white lotuses. Vishnu and Lakshami sit amid the white lotuses, where they both radiate like the Sun.

Vishnu's role as preserver seems to have developed as a means to maintain balance in the universe between good and evil powers. In the normal course of events, the gods and demons are evenly matched in the world. At times, however, demons seem to gain the upper hand. During such times, Vishnu, as preserver, intervenes to restore balance by descending to Earth in the form of an incarnation. "Whenever the Sacred Law fails, and evil raises its head, I [Vishnu] take embodied birth. To guard the righteous, to root out sinners, and to establish the Sacred Law, I am born from age to age." (Bhagavad Gita IV.6-8)

Hindu mythology holds that there are 10 incarnations of Vishnu, called *avatars.* During each incarnation, Vishnu has a specific task to perform. Of the 10 avatars, four are animals. In the form of *matsya* (a fish), Vishnu saved the sage Manu and the sacred Vedas from a great flood. Also in this flood, the gods lost

■ *The beneficent god Vishnu reclines on the thousand-headed primordial serpent. From his navel emerges Brahma, the world creator. The world created by Brahma is ruled by Vishnu for a **yuga** (a long period of time), after which it is dissolved and re-created. Thus the cycle of **samsara** goes on.*

for a time the elixir of their immortality. Vishnu assumed the form of *kurma,* a great tortoise, and dove to the bottom of the ocean to retrieve the potent drink.

When the demon *Hiranyaksha* cast the earth to the bottom of the sea, Vishnu became *varaha,* the boar. He plunged into the depths, saved the earth and spread it on top of the waters to float. Another demon, the tyrant *Hiranyakashapa,* had obtained a special privilege through which he could be killed neither by human nor animal, neither inside nor outside of his home, nor by day nor by night. He lived without fear and wreaked great havoc wherever he went. To overcome the demon, Vishnu took the form of the *narasimha* (half human and half lion) and killed Hiranyakashapa on the threshold of his home at sunset.

Other avatars were human in form. A popular legend told of the three great strides with which Vishnu stepped over the universe and foiled the demon-king, *Bali.* The demon-king had control of the Earth, so Vishnu devised a plan to deceive the king. Vishnu took the form of *Vamana,* the dwarf, and asked the king if he could have as much space as he could cover in three steps. Believing that the dwarf could only cover a small space, Bali agreed. Then Vishnu became Vamana, a great giant, and strode across the earth and the heavens. At another time, the Kshatriyas (the warrior class) threatened to oust the Brahmins from power. So Vishnu was born as the Brahmin Parashurama, known as *Rama* with the Axe, to assert the sanctity of the caste system.

Traditionally, the ninth avatar of Vishnu was the religious sage, the *Buddha.* Some Hindu texts state that Vishnu, as the Buddha, taught wrong religious ideas to evil people. Other texts claim that the Buddha was born to save innocent animals, as part of his doctrine of nonviolence to all living things.

The tenth avatar is the only incarnation of Vishnu that is yet to come. It is believed that this manifestation of the great god, referred to as *Kalki,* will appear at the "end" of the present time, riding a white horse and holding a flaming sword.

All ten avatars were recognized in the sacred scriptures by around the 11th century C.E. By far, however, the most widely worshipped of these gods were Rama and *Krishna,* the seventh and eighth avatars of Vishnu.

■ *This drawing depicts the emblems that are always carried by Vishnu: a discus, a club, a lotus, and a conch shell.*

The Adventures of Rama, Prince of Ayodhya

Rama, the prince of Ayodha, was the seventh avatar of Vishnu. The great epic poem the *Ramayana* (adventures of Rama) tells of Rama's life. As we have said, Rama's task in this incarnation was to subdue the powerful 10-headed Ravana, demon-king of Sri Lanka. The demon-king's demise is the central theme of the *Ramayana.*

The king Ravana was said to be a devoted student of Vedic rituals. Brahma rewarded his devotion with a gift of invulnerability. Ravana could be killed neither by god nor demon. However, Ravana misused the gift of Brahma; he conquered the heavens and brought all the gods to Sri Lanka where they served him in chains. Indra became his wreath maker, Brahma his messenger, Agni his cook, Vishnu his steward, Shiva his barber, Vayu his sweeper, and Varuna his water carrier. Thus Ravana's uncompromising devotion to the god Brahma was so profound that it shook the foundations of the celestial, atmospheric, and earthly worlds.

The gods appealed to Vishnu for a solution to their predicament. Vishnu declared that Ravana had been too proud to ask for immunity from mere mortals. As a result, he would be slain because of a woman, by a human, and aided by animals. Then Vishnu incarnated himself as Rama, a mere mortal. However, he was the oldest son of the king Dasratha. Through the story of Rama's life, we are led to the king's demise.

Rama married a princess named Sita. Shortly after the marriage, Dasratha decided to retire and make his son Rama king. Dasratha's queen, however, asked the king for a favor he had promised to her long before. She asked that her son Bharata take the throne as king, and that Rama be exiled for fourteen years. Dasratha was utterly disheartened, but he kept his word.

Rama wanted to go into exile alone, but his wife Sita and his brother and best friend, Lakshamana, insisted on accompanying him. So, with all the loyal subjects lamenting their departure, the three companions set off into the forest. Rama's father, Dasratha, died of grief within a few days.

In the meantime, Bharata was returning from a journey for what he thought was to be the coronation of his brother, Rama. When he learned what had happened, he was appalled. Bharata went to the forest to persuade his elder brother to return to the throne. However, Rama politely refused, saying that he could not oppose his father's word. Bharata returned to the kingdom but reigned only as a viceroy, preserving a pair of Rama's sandals on the throne as a symbol of the rightful king.

The demon-king Ravana's sister, Surpanakha, often visited the forest where Rama, Sita, and Lakshamana lived. She fell in love with Rama, but he resisted her advances because he loved Sita. Angered, Surpanakha turned her affections toward Lakshamana. Lakshamana ignored her completely. When she persisted, he became very annoyed and cut off her nose and ears.

Surpanakha was crazed. She decided to entice her brother, Ravana, with details of Sita's beauty. She told him what a perfect wife Sita would be for him. Ravana was intrigued, but he was also well aware of Rama's power. Ravana knew that it would be most difficult to take Sita from Rama.

To get Sita, Ravana sent an enchanted deer to the forest. This deer was so beautiful that Sita asked Rama and Lakshamana to catch it for her. While the two brothers chased the deer, Ravana disguised himself as an ascetic. He approached Sita and took her away in his chariot to his golden palace in Sri Lanka. On the way, Jatayu, Rama's bird friend, saw them. He tried to save Sita but was mortally wounded.

Meanwhile, the two brothers returned from their quest to capture the enchanted deer. They found Jatayu and learned from the wounded bird what had happened. Greatly disturbed, Rama made plans to rescue Sita. He made an alliance with the monkey-king Sugriva, who presented Rama with an army of monkeys and bears. The general of this army was the mighty *Hanuman,* son of *Vayu,* the wind god. Before anyone else could reach Sri Lanka, Hanuman had flown to Ravana's palace and found Sita alone in a garden. He gave her Rama's ring as a token and assured her that Rama would rescue her. However, Hanuman was caught by Ravana's guards, who brought him before the demon-king. Ravana ordered the guards to wrap oily rags around Hanuman's tail and to set fire to them. But Hanuman managed to escape, jumping from building to building with his burning tail trailing behind him. He set fire to all the buildings of the golden palace.

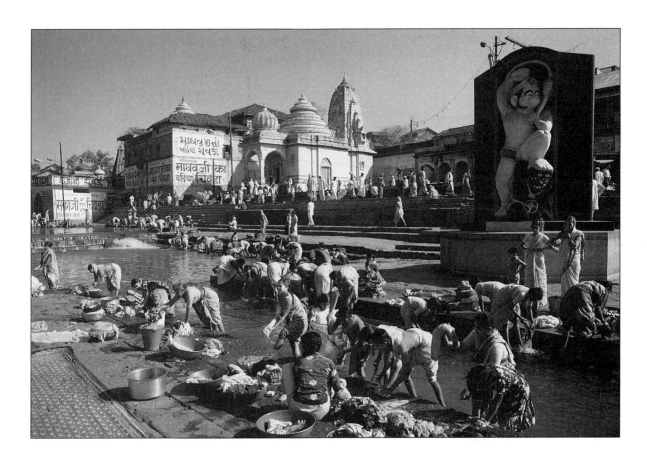

Because he was able to fly, Hanuman flew back to the mainland where he rejoined Rama. Upon hearing Hanuman's story, Rama went to Sri Lanka with the monkey army, and a mighty battle was fought before the gates of the city. During the battle Hanuman, with golden skin, red face, and enormous tail, was terrifyingly valiant. But his greatest service was his flight to the Himalayas from which he brought herbs to cure Rama and Lakshamana when they were wounded.

The forces of Ravana fought vigorously, but all the demons, including Ravana's two brothers, were killed. Finally, Rama and Ravana faced each other in combat. The Earth trembled as they fought, and the whole company of gods watched. At one point, Rama felt that Ravana had begun to overpower him. Rama drew out the dreaded brahmastra, a magic weapon fused with the

■ *A huge Hanuman (the monkey god) relief on the banks of the Nasik River overlooks washermen. Hanuman is the symbol of an ideal devotee and of renunciation.*

energy of many gods. He strung the weapon on his bow and, whispering a Vedic mantra, shot it toward Ravana and killed him. At that moment, all the gods showered Rama with wreaths. Rama and Sita were reunited and returned to their kingdom with Lakshamana and Hanuman.

It is said that during Rama's reign, the world knew unprecedented peace. However, the people of his kingdom began to gossip about Sita. They charged that because she had lived in Ravana's palace she might not be fit to be the queen. The people mistrusted Sita, so Rama felt obliged to send his queen into exile, even though she was pregnant at the time. She took refuge in a forest hermitage where she gave birth to twin sons, Luv and Kush.

When the twins were 15 years old, they went to visit the capital and were recognized by their father. Rama then sent for Sita. He called together a great assembly so that Sita could publicly declare her innocence. In front of the assembly, Sita called upon Earth, her mother (for Sita had been born in a furrow), to prove her innocence. The Earth opened and swallowed her into its womb. Rama was heartbroken and wished to follow her. He walked into the river, where Brahma's voice welcomed him into heaven.

For Hindus, the characters of the *Ramayana* are models of human existence. Rama was not only a just king but an ideal son for having honored his father's promise. Sita was an ideal wife because she gave up queenly comforts to be with her husband. Lakshamana was a model brother who, like Sita, left the comforts of royalty to support Rama. Hanuman was the ideal devotee who followed and served faithfully. All of these characters are celebrated in Hindu households and frequently mentioned in Hindu sacred and secular literature.

Krishna

One of Hinduism's most widely worshipped gods is Krishna, the eighth avatar of Vishnu. His popularity may be due in part to his extremely colorful character. From his childhood, Krishna performed many great feats. As a youth, he dallied with milkmaids. As a young man, he performed the task for which he was incarnated. And in middle age, as a great ruler, he took part in the mythological Mahabharata War, which is described in the great epic *Mahabharata.*

The story of Krishna starts with the demon Kansa, a tyrant who usurped the throne of his own father, Ugrasena, and imprisoned him. Kansa had heard from a sage that a son of one of his female kin would bring about his demise. So, the demon-king ordered all her children to be slain. Immediately, six children were put to death. However, her seventh child, Balarama, and her eighth child, Krishna, were miraculously saved and secretly given to foster parents. When Kansa learned of their escapes, he ordered a massacre. Again the brothers were saved. Nanda and Yasoda, Krishna's foster parents, fled to Gokula and reared the boys among the milkmaids and cowherds.

In early childhood, Krishna revealed a dual character. Sometimes, he was a normal, lovable baby. At other times, he exhibited extraordinary superhuman strength. One popular myth tells of Krishna's encounter with the demon Putna, an ogress who, disguised as a beautiful girl, would suckle babies with her poisoned breasts. But her poison could not harm Krishna—he sucked so hard that he drew all the life out of Putna. The youthful Krishna often amused himself by playing pranks on his adoptive mother and the milkmaids of Gokula. He stole curds and butter, raided orchards for fruit, upset pails of milk, and blamed the other children for all his mischief.

As a young man, Krishna is renowned for his amorous adventures with numerous maidens. One tale tells of his encounter with a hunchbacked, ugly maiden, Kubja, who was bearing perfumed oils for tyrant-demon Kansa. When Krishna asked her for some of the perfume, she rubbed it on his body. In return, Krishna pressed on her feet with his own foot, lifted her chin, and straightened her. Other adventures with a milkmaid named Radha are told in stories noted for their beauty and sensuous descriptions. These stories also have a spiritual meaning because in them, Krishna symbolizes the universal soul, and the milkmaids are individual souls longing to be united with the Ultimate Reality and achieve enlightenment.

All through Krishna's growing years, Kansa continued to plot his death, but Krishna was always able to fend off the

■ *The love of cowherd Krishna and his beloved Radha is celebrated in hundreds of Hindu songs and stories. Their love symbolizes the longing of devotees for their personal deities.*

tyrant's attempts. Krishna destroyed the snake demon Kaliya by dancing on his head. He also swallowed a fire demon sent to consume the young god and his companions.

Finally, the demon-king Kansa masterminded a plot to slay both Krishna and his brother Balarama. To kill them, he would host a series of athletic games and invite them both. On their way to the court of Mathura where the games would be held, Krishna and Balarama encountered many of Kansa's cohorts—demons and monsters and ogres. Krishna and Balarama thwarted these evil beings, just as they did the host of gruesome demons that appeared at the games. Finally, Kansa himself opposed Krishna, only to have the prophecy of the sage come true: Krishna slayed Kansa. Having done so, Krishna restored Ugrasena, the rightful king, to the throne. He also traveled to the underworld to bring back to life the six brothers who were killed by Kansa at birth.

Then Krishna abandoned the pastoral life and became a feudal prince, thus entering the last phase of his life.

Krishna's struggles with the forces of evil climaxed in the Mahabharata War between his kinsmen, the Pandavas and the Kauravas. In a prewar council, Krishna tried to reconcile the opposing parties, but to no avail. Then, since he had promised not to participate actively in the skirmish, Krishna disguised himself as the charioteer of Arjuna, a member of the Pandava family. Arjuna asked his charioteer to draw up to a point from which they could survey the battlefield. While looking down on the opposed forces of his family, Arjuna questioned the reasoning of kinsmen killing kinsmen.

Krishna's response to Arjuna—contained in the well-known Hindu scripture, the Bhagavad Gita—regards religious obligation and devotion to God. In his discussion, Krishna informs Arjuna of the higher universal order to which he must be true—that which is beyond the temporary existence of this world. He points out that Arjuna is of the warrior caste and that he must fulfill his duty as a warrior. Krishna also tells Arjuna that though his body may die, his soul is indestructible.

Stories of Krishna appear in many Hindu texts, but the most well-known and respected of these are the teachings found in the Bhagavad Gita. The Bhagavad Gita is a very short section (about 18 chapters) of the 100,000 verses of the *Mahabharata*. Teachings in the Bhagavad Gita are revered by Hindus of many sects. Many Hindus have memorized verses from the Gita, and often parts of the Gita are spoken during daily devotions. The teachings of the Gita are spoken by Krishna in this scripture whose author is unknown.

Instead of bringing out differences among the various systems of Hindu thought and practice, the Bhagavad Gita emphasizes the points of agreement among them. It thereby brings about a religious and philosophical unity. It discusses *sva-dharma,* the individual's duties or social obligations. It stresses the significance of all the castes. Furthermore, this text recommends total devotion, or bhakti, as the most effective form of religion. It assumes that there is a personal god who blesses with divine grace the devoted worshippers.

In the Bhagavad Gita, Krishna describes his relation to his devotees:

A leaf, a flower, a fruit, or water
whoever offers to me with devotion—
that same, proffered in devotion by
one whose soul is pure, I accept.

Even if a person of extremely vile conduct
worships me being devoted to none else,
he is to be reckoned as righteous, for he
has engaged himself in action in the right
spirit. Quickly does he become of righteous
soul and obtains eternal peace. Know for
certain that my devotee perishes not.

For those who take refuge in me,
even though they be lowly born, women,
vaisyas (the third Hindu caste), and
also sudras (the lowest Hindu caste)
even they attain to the highest goal.

Arjuna's relationship with Krishna existed on many levels. He was Krisha's warrior and student, and he was completely devoted to him. Arjuna's devotion to Krisha was intensified when Krishna revealed to him his awesome forms—as all gods, Brahman, the soul of the world. Thus Arjuna's chief feelings for Krishna were awe inspired:

You (Krishna) are the father of the universe,
of all that moves and all that moves not,
its worshipful and worthy teacher.
You have no equal—what in the three worlds
could equal you 0 power beyond compare?

So, reverently prostrating my body,
I crave your grace, 0 blessed lord
As father to son, as friend to friend,
as lover to beloved, bear with me, god.

The relationship Arjuna had with Krishna is an example of an individual having a personal god. This kind of relationship is further elaborated by poet-sages throughout India from the eighth to the 16th centuries. These writers have produced widely popular literature.

Krishna and Balarama spent the last days of their lives in a forest refuge where Balarama died in his sleep. Krishna mourned alone under a fig tree on the bank of a river but a passing hunter mistook him for a deer and wounded him fatally.

The Supreme Goddess Mahadevi Shakti

Goddesses have been revered since the pre-Aryan time of the Indus Valley culture, when devotees attributed the fertility of the land to a maternal deity. By the Vedic period, significant female deities had emerged. These include *Prithvi,* the goddess earth, and Vac, the goddess of speech and wisdom.

In the epics, the consorts—*Sarasvati,* Parvati, and Lakshami—of the three major gods had become quite prominent in themselves. Sarasvati (associated with Vac) is regarded as the goddess of all the creative arts, sciences, and knowledge. Parvati, the wife of Shiva, is associated with the Himalayas. Like her husband, she has immense ascetic and erotic characteristics. Lakshami, Vishnu's consort, is associated with the lotus, symbol of power and good luck.

Though these goddesses came to hold much respect in the minds of goddess devotees, the great goddess Mahadevi Shakti is the one ultimate reality. In addition to the three major goddesses, numerous minor goddesses are revered by Hindus. However, all the goddesses are manifestations of Mahadevi, the great goddess. With the popularity of the sixth-century *Markandya Purana,* worship of the great goddess had become well established. At present, goddess worship is visible primarily in the villages, and many of these goddesses have only local reputations. In the minds of villagers, all these local goddesses are associated with the great goddess, Mahadevi Shakti.

Mahadevi is an active and powerful female, who is attentive to the stability of the world and to the needs of her devotees. She is worshipped for her different aspects, including those of the great maternal goddess and the devoted consort or wife. Her character has a beneficent side as well as a destructive side. Hindus perceive the two sides of Mahadevi as a natural part of an orderly universe containing both positive and negative forces—life and death, creation and destruction, vigor and rest.

The complexity of Mahadevi Shakti—in such forms as *Sati*, Parvati, *Durga*, and *Kali*—is expressed in a variety of roles that she shares with her husband, Shiva. She is both mild and fierce. In her mild form she is Sati, daughter of a sage who marries Shiva against her father's wishes. Later she sacrifices herself on her father's sacrificial fire because he does not approve of Shiva, her husband. After some time, Sati is reborn as Parvati, the daughter of *Himavat*, god of mountains. She practices austere yoga. Shiva is impressed by her yogic powers and marries her again.

In her fierce form, the great goddess is Durga. Durga was created out of angry flames that issued forth from the mouths of Brahma, Vishnu, Shiva, and other gods. She was specifically

■ *The Great Goddess Shakti, or Devi. Like Shiva, Shakti is both auspicious as well as terrifying. Here she is shown in her auspicious form, surrounded by major Hindu gods: Brahma, Vishnu, Shiva, and Surya (the sun god).*

created by the gods to kill the buffalo demon, Mahisha, who, by abstinence, had gained the strength to drive the gods from their celestial kingdom.

Durga was born fully grown and beautiful, riding a tiger from the Himalayan forests. She was immediately armed by the gods, and in each of her 10 hands she held special weapons: Vishnu's discus, Shiva's trident (three-pronged spear), Agni's flaming dart, Indra's thunderbolt, and Varuna's conch shell, among others. With these weapons, Durga killed the buffalo-demon and returned the gods to their rightful kingdom.

On another occasion, the gods appealed to the goddess Durga to eliminate the demon brothers Sumbha and Nisumbha. Shiva had blessed the brothers with immortality because they had performed austerities that made the gods tremble. As a goddess capable of defeating demons, Durga agreed to combat the brothers. When she appeared before Sumbha, his passion was aroused, and he desired to possess her. She agreed to consent only if he could overcome her in battle. Sumbha accepted the condition unhesitatingly, not realizing that the immortality granted him was protection from gods only, and not from goddesses. And so Durga defeated the demon and his brother with ease.

Despite her grace, Durga combatted many demons who had obtained boons protecting them from gods and men. Her primary role was to maintain and protect cosmic order by appearing periodically to battle such demon oppressors.

Kali, "the black one," personifies the most terrifying aspects of Mahadevi Shakti. She leaves bloodshed, disease, and death in her wake. Her body is decked with terrible ornaments made from bones; a string of human skulls adorns her neck. She wields a sword in one hand, a dagger in another, and the severed heads of two giants hang, dripping blood, from her two other hands. Her hair is wildly disheveled, tusks protrude from her face, a third eye peers out from the middle of her forehead, and she is often portrayed with her tongue hanging out. Having overcome the power of death, she dwells in the cremation ground, seating herself on corpses.

One myth tells of how Kali rid the world of the dreaded tyrant Raktabija. Wherever a drop of his blood fell, thousands of demons would appear. Thus Kali slew him and drained all the blood from his body.

With all her gruesome characteristics, Kali became an ultimate representation of death. Many Hindus believe that spiritual enlightenment can be achieved if the terrifying aspects of this deity, the image of all life's fear and pain, can be overcome.

Through centuries of change, an often expanding pantheon of Hindu goddesses and gods encompassed a broad range of disparate beliefs. Common among the philosophies and sects that emerged was a goal to perceive the ultimate reality on a more personal level than had previously been thought possible. This desire grew in popularity and blossomed into an influential movement based on personal devotion to an individual deity.

Bhakti, or Devotion

The most important theme throughout the epics and the *Puranas* was that of bhakti, or devotion. Early bhakti reflected the cultural and social changes that were taking place in Hindu society before and during Islamic rule. The bhakti movement expressed a great change from traditionally Vedic-based ceremonies and attitudes, although the authority of the Vedas was never renounced. More recent religious texts stress the independence of bhakti religion from other means of salvation.

bhakti was conceived as a way of life, a selfless and complete surrender to God. Members of the movement invoked their goddess or god by name and recited hymns of praise, always being mindful of the deity. Devotees were to acknowledge no difference between themselves and others. They were required to be free of jealousy, falsehood, envy, and injury. Nor were bhakti devotees encouraged to take pride in their birthright or wealth. The teachings of bhakti implied that a person's birth and caste had no significant influence on their salvation—salvation depended only on a devotee's purity of heart.

Devotional emphasis also carried over into social attitudes. Material poverty was looked on with favor. Great compassion was shown for the persecuted, distressed, and despised. And caste distinctions were declared irrelevant. Women have played significant roles in the Hindu tradition as mothers and wives;

however, throughout Indian history, whenever women were able to break away from social and religious customs, they have magnificently contributed to various other fields of life. In the area of religion, two women who come to mind are the saint-poetesses of the bhakti movement: Lalleshwari (14th century) and Mira Bhai (16th century).

The writers of the bhakti movement (eighth to 17th centuries) chose to write in languages spoken by the common people of local regions. This was because Sanskrit, the language of the *Puranas,* was only taught to the learned of the Brahmin caste. Sanskrit was the language of the elite, even though in earlier times it contained some popular expressions that may have come from some less-educated people. The bhakti writers chose not to write in Sanskrit to make their literature most accessible.

The language of devotion was the language of human emotion, at times so intense that it was painful, highly moving, and intensely personal. The poet-sages related their relationship with God in terms of love, friendship, despair, and joy. They implied that the goal of bhakti was salvation in very personal terms, not merely an ambiguous union with the impersonal Brahman (Universal Soul). Salvation through bhakti included an eternal relationship of blissful devotion. In this relationship, unlike that pictured by the earlier ascetics, the devotee and the Ultimate Reality would remain separate. In the words of one poet, devotion was "to taste sugar, not become sugar."

Intense devotional fervor was evident in the poetry of the movement. The poets produced thousands of poems in various regional languages. The poets belonged to the people and integrated them by conveying this religious movement from region to region. Though they themselves were from different social levels of Hindu society, the poets helped keep Brahmanism alive. They constantly revitalized Hindu ideas and beliefs, making this religion available to all people.

Because of this facilitating role, poets who possessed outstanding powers of expression became quite popular all over India. An eighth-century poet from the south of India wrote:

I am false, my heart is false, my love is false,
But I, this sinner, can win thee if I weep before thee, O lord,

Thou who art sweet like
honey, nectar, and the juice of sugar cane!
Please bless me so that I can reach thee.

Lalleshwari, the 14th-century Kashmiri devotional poetess wrote in opposition to temple worship:

Image is of stone, temple is of stone, Above and Below are
one, which of them will you worship, O foolish Pandit?
Because within you lies the union of mind and soul.

She mocked religious persecution and discrimination, saying:

Shiva permeates this Universe
Do not discriminate between a Hindu and a Muslim
If thou art sharp enough, know thyself.

Some have abandoned home
some the forest abode
What use the hermitage if thou controllest not thine mind.

Basavanna, a 12th-century devotional poet from South India, offered his body to his personal god because he, unlike rich devotees, could not afford to build a temple:

The rich
will make temples for Shiva
What shall I,
a poor man do?

My legs are pillars,
the body the shrine,
the head a cupola of gold.

Listen, O Lord,
things standing shall fall,
but the moving ever shall stay.

In this poem, the poet's body is compared with a temple. He reminds us that the temple has become a meaningless monument with its original symbolism forgotten. By identifying his body with a temple, the poet makes his body sacred, and he offers himself to God. He emphasizes that rich people only make temples, but poor people themselves become temples, exhibiting the intensity and purity of their devotion.

Poet-sages were considered godlike humans who not only continued Hindu traditions throughout Muslim rule but spread it throughout India, integrating local traditions into a national religion. They were considered a link between the human and the divine and were symbols of the Hindu idea that an element of the sacred dwells within each individual.

It was because of devout saints that all the Hindu religious sects were woven together in a complex system. However, political integration did not follow social and cultural integration. In 712 C.E., a 21-year-old Arab military leader named Muhammad ibn Kasim swept into the Indus Valley, introducing the challenge of Islam and eras of change that would alter the face of Hinduism forever.

CHAPTER 5

Political and Social Change

*T*he eighth century C.E. brought the beginning of an endless series of changes and challenges to India and to Hinduism. With new religions, new rulers, new laws, and new saints, Hinduism proved to be a stable and flexible religious way of life.

Islam in India

Islam came to India first as a religion, then as a political force. In the eighth century, Arabs infiltrated the Indian continent. Almost three centuries later, the Afghans, the Turks, and the Persians, all Muslims, came to conquer but stayed as the rulers. By the thirteenth century, Muslim rule had blossomed throughout most of northern India. The cultural and the political center of the new rulers was Delhi.

The Islamic culture in India reached its height under the Mughal Empire. The Mughal dynasty was founded by a Persian warrior chief named Babur in the early 16th century. The empire reached its apex of brilliance during the reign of Babur's great-grandson Akbar the Great (r. 1556–1605). By the beginning of the 18th century, however, it had declined.

Muslim rulers dominated India for almost nine centuries, Hindus responded to this domination in a variety of ways. Some converted to Islam, but the majority remained loyal to their religious heritage. Life was difficult for Hindus under Muslim rule. Muslim rulers imposed a special tax on non-Muslims. In addition, they demolished Hindu temples and destroyed countless idols. The Muslims considered the Hindus to be pagans, and they especially despised the Hindu tradition of image worship. As a result, an enduring hostility arose between the two groups.

For the most part, Hindus and Muslims did not interact. However, poet-sages of the era drew on both religions, and Muslims supported scholars and artists, among whom Hindus numbered significantly. As a result, Hinduism was influenced by Islam, and Islam by Hinduism. Some influences were more direct. The Muslims stifled the elitist Brahmanic traditions but allowed devotional movements such as bhakti to flourish. Islamic mysticism, or Sufism, had much in common with the Hindu bhakti movement. Both emphasized a direct personal relationship with God. Together they produced a religious outlook whose outstanding aspect was its movement away from organized sects and orthodox scriptures and toward devotional worship.

One of the most popular poet-sages of the era was Kabir. Raised a Muslim, Kabir was influenced by Sufism and later embraced Hinduism. His teachings emphasized love of God and the idea that God would return that love despite caste and creed. Kabir's writings convey the simple nature of devotional worship:

> I do not ring the temple bell,
> I do not set the idol on its throne,
> I do not worship the image with flowers
> It is not the austerities that mortify the flesh
> which are pleasing to the lord,
> When you leave off your clothes and kill your senses,
> you do not please the lord.
> The man who is kind and who practices righteousness,
> who remains passive amidst the affairs of the world,
> who considers all creatures on earth as his own self,
> He attains the Immortal Being, the true God is ever with him.

By the time the Mughal emperor Akbar came to power in the 16th century, there was an active sea route between Europe and India. In the 1540s, Saint Francis Xavier founded a Christian mission on Indian shores. The priests tried to convert Akbar, who became curious not only about Christianity but other religions as well. He tried to introduce religious tolerance, for example, by lifting the tax on non-Muslims. Akbar's successor, however, reimposed the tax and devastated many Hindu temples.

British Rule

By 1700, the Mughal Empire was in decline. By this time, India's coasts were dotted with European trading settlements and missionary centers. The British moved to protect their interests in India by establishing colonies. Within 50 years, the British East India Company had gained control over India's most prosperous provinces. By 1818, the British were in control of the entire Indian subcontinent, including present-day India, Pakistan, Bangladesh, and Sri Lanka.

British rule brought enormous changes in Indian life. The British introduced Western education so that increasing numbers of people became literate. Occupations formerly reserved for one caste or class became open to all. Secular laws diminished the authority of the Hindu religious code. British rule thus disrupted and changed some of the basic ideas of Hinduism. It also altered the society in which Hindus had lived. Jobs in industry and business moved people to the cities. Many people found themselves free of traditional family-centered religious and social obligations they had taken for granted.

At the beginning of British rule, the Indian population spoke fourteen different literary languages and hundreds of dialects. British officials moved quickly to make English the dominant language in the schools and colleges. Public education was suddenly open to all. Christian missionaries came to India and opened schools and colleges for both women and men. Christianity challenged Hindu customs that had existed for centuries.

One such custom was the caste system, which justified hereditary occupations and unequal distribution of opportunities.

■ *Hindu women, like Hindu men, are being educated in arts and modern sciences at universities. Although the number of educated women is not as high as that of men, it is growing every year.*

Hindus considered the caste system to be part of the normal course of life. The miserable conditions of the lower classes were also considered normal. Women suffered under harsh codes that forced them into marriage as young girls and denied remarriage to widows, no matter how young they were. The practice of *sati* required a wife to burn herself to death on the funeral pyre of her husband.

As a result of Western influence, many Indians began to doubt the traditions of Hinduism. Educated Hindus became uncomfortable with their religion after comparing it to the ethical standards of the Western countries. At the same time, however, European scholars were researching India's forgotten past. They uncovered records of a greater pre-Islamic India in which brilliant systems of thought were developed and great works of literature and art were created. Hindu religious leaders called on young people to identify with that ancient heritage and its rich cultural and spiritual resources.

Consequently, by the end of the 19th century, a passionate nationalism with religious overtones began to grow in the minds of educated Indians. While recognizing that the Western countries led in science and technology, they had come to see the East as the world's center of spiritual culture. A number of prominent Hindu figures emerged at this time to lead their religion into reform.

Rammohan Roy (1772–1833)

Rammohan Roy is called the father of modern India. Born of devout Brahmin parents in Bengal, he showed an intense interest in religion from his early years. He studied the Upanishadic scriptures, which he considered the core of Hinduism. Roy joined the British civil service and rose as high as was possible for an Indian at the time. He retired at 42 and settled in Calcutta, then the political and intellectual capital of India.

As a young man, Roy had witnessed the death of his sister-in-law in the act of sati. She was forced onto her husband's funeral pyre and held there with long poles while the sound of drums drowned out her screams. Horrified by this experience, Roy became a vehement opponent of sati. He founded several newspapers, which he published in different languages. He campaigned against sati, child marriage, image worship, and other Hindu customs he felt were misguided. Roy denounced polytheism, the worship of many gods. He founded a religious society, *Brahmo Samaj* (Society of God). Its members gathered weekly for congregational-style meetings in which people prayed, sang hymns, and listened to sermons based on the Hindu scriptures.

Debendranath Tagore (1817–1905)

After Roy's death, the Brahmo Samaj (Brahmos) leadership fell to Debendranath Tagore. Tagore had begun with a group of his own, which he merged with Roy's in 1843. Like Roy's group, Tagore's opposed image worship. Under Tagore, Brahmos declared that the final authority in religion was to be found in human reason and conscience, not in ancient scriptures. Its members were asked to give up their caste identities. They fought against child marriage and the tradition of having more than one wife. The group had a significant impact during the second half of the 19th century, Then a rift between Tagore and one of the group's members, Keshab Chandra Sen, weakened its influence. Sen began discussion groups and schools, advocated the remarriage of widows, and encouraged the education of women, but he and Tagore differed on the wearing of the sacred thread, a sign of Brahmin birth. Tagore withdrew from the Brahmos and devoted himself to continuing the work Roy had begun, particularly reviving Hindu monotheism.

Dayanada Sarasvati (1824–1883)

Dayanada Sarasvati was born into a wealthy Brahmin family. The deaths of his sister and his uncle when he was a young man led him to ponder the problems of life and afterlife. He renounced the world and became an ascetic. Study of the scriptures turned him away from the popular gods of Hinduism. Later, his experiences while traveling throughout India caused him to question many Hindu customs.

In 1860, Sarasvati became the student of Swami Virajananda, a blind Vedic scholar. The truths he found in the Vedas led him to vow opposition to the corruptions of Hinduism. He began by lecturing in Sanskrit, but in 1874 he began to speak in Hindi, the language of the common people. The following year, he founded the *Arya Samaj* (Noble Society).

Like Rammohan Roy, Sarasvati rejected Hindu polytheism. He considered the Vedas the only authority for Hindu belief. He denounced child marriage, the subjugation of women by men, and the worship of images, all of which are not recommended in the Vedas. Moreover, he said that Hindu castes had no place in true Hindu religion. There should be no untouchable caste; names for castes should not be used to designate birth status.

Sarasvati considered Hinduism to be the only true religion. He did not believe in tolerance of other religions, which he said were corruptions of the monotheism of the Vedas. He considered conversions to other religions, especially Christianity, intolerable. His society also fought against foreign cultural influences. This theme continues in the reform movements of today.

Ramakrishna (1836–1886)

Ramakrishna was the son of a village priest. From the age of seven, he experienced mystic trances and divine visions. He often meditated before the image of Kali, the great mother goddess in her terrible form, imagining that she was breathing and listening to him. One day, he believed, the goddess revealed herself to him. From that time on, her image or the sound of her name would send him into a trance.

Ramakrishna became an ascetic, devoting himself to prayer and meditation. Later he became a meditating yogi. He worshipped like a bhakti devotee and explored Buddhism and Shaktism (worship of the goddess Shakti).

Ramakrishna came to believe that all religions were glorifications of the same entity. He studied Islam and meditated on Muhammad until Muhammad appeared to him in a vision. Then he read the Bible and meditated on pictures of the Madonna and Child until a vision of Christ appeared to him. He declared that all religions were equally effective ways of coming into contact with divinity.

In the last years of his life, Ramakrishna gathered a group of disciples around him. One of these was a young law student who became his successor.

■ *All love is expansion, all selfishness is contraction. Love is therefore the only law of life. He who loves lives; he who is selfish is dying. Therefore, love for love's sake, because it is the law of life, just as you breathe to live.*

—Vivekananda

Vivekananda (1863–1902)

Vivekananda was planning to study law in England when he met Ramakrishna. He abandoned his plans for a legal career and became an ascetic. In 1893, he traveled to Chicago for the Parliament of Religions, where he spoke for Hinduism. There he declared, "All religions are one." Vivekananda traveled in America and England before returning to India, where he devoted the rest of his life to helping the poor and to religious education. His greatest achievement was that of reviving interest in Hinduism throughout the world.

Rabindranath Tagore (1861–1941)

Rabindranath Tagore was the 14th of the 15 children of Debendranath Tagore, the leader of the Brahmo Samaj. Tagore began writing poetry at 13, and at 20, he published his first

■ *Rabindranath Tagore with his daughter in Romania. Tagore wrote in English as well as in Bengali. He rejected the Hindu idea of the world as illusion (**maya**). His poems celebrate the beauties and bounties of nature and human freedom.*

volume of Bengali poems. Over the next 30 years, as he continued to write poetry, his writing matured in style and deepened in content. In 1912, Tagore published *Gitanjali* (Song offering) following the deaths of his wife and three of his five children. A year later, he received the Nobel Prize in literature, awarded each year to only one writer as a tribute to that writer's lifetime achievement and considered the highest honor a writer can receive.

Tagore founded a school at Shantiniketan, Bengal, for creative and performing artists. In 1921, he expanded his retreat into a university, which he dedicated to his ideal of world brotherhood and cultural exchange. Tagore felt that nationalism and materialism were great evils. He believed that the best hope for humanity was to return to the spiritual values found in all religions. Tagore saw India as the spiritual teacher of the world, but he valued the West's vitality and search for truth.

One of Tagore's contemporaries was Mohandas Gandhi, who was attaining widespread recognition as head of a movement to oppose everything British. Tagore disagreed strongly with Gandhi and his methods. He felt that politics distracted people from more important issues, such as erasing caste barriers, uplifting the poor and helpless, and reconciling Hindus and Muslims. But despite their ideological differences, Rabindranath Tagore recognized Gandhi's greatness. It was he who first called Gandhi *Mahatma*, an honorary title meaning "the Great Soul."

Mohandas Gandhi (1869–1948) and the Indian National Movement

India had been under British rule for almost half a century when Mohandas Gandhi was born in 1869. Gandhi grew up in a traditional, middle-class Hindu family. At 19, he went to London to study law, returning to India in 1891. Shy and retiring, he found little success in the practice of law. In 1893, he accepted a job offer in South Africa. There he experienced firsthand the prejudices held by white South Africans against Indians.

Gandhi's law job in South Africa ended after one year, but for the next 21 years, he remained there working for Indian rights. Drawing on his fundamental Hindu beliefs, he developed what he called *satyagraha*—nonviolent social action. Satyagraha was based on Hindu principles of truth, nonviolence, and courage. Gandhi taught that the practice of *satyagraha* in the face of injustice would bring about social change.

Gandhi returned to India in 1915. There he became leader of the Indian nationalist movement, which aimed at freeing India from British rule. Gandhi set up training centers at which he taught *satyagraha* and also life skills to help India's downtrodden poor to become self-sufficient. He renounced worldly life and possessions and devoted himself wholly to moving India toward independence. He led uprisings against British rule, even going to prison for his beliefs. Many people believed that Gandhi was divinely inspired; others came to see him as the god Vishnu returned. With great moral and political power on his side, Gandhi and his followers overcame Britain's hold on the country, and Britain agreed to withdraw from India. On August 15, 1947, India became independent.

Partition

The end of British rule had its costs, however. For many years, an uneasy political situation had existed between the Hindus, mostly concentrated in the south and the west, and the Muslims, to the north. The two groups had not only different religious views but also different social and political aims. Each mistrusted the other. Under the British, they were held together by their mutual struggle against foreign domination. With independence on the horizon, their differences became even more pronounced. Although the British wanted to maintain India as one country with different self-governing regions, they also suggested that if the Hindus and Muslims could not agree, they might separate into two different countries. The British would leave it up to the people to decide.

When the British withdrew, uprisings broke out all over India. Many thousands of people died, and several million more became refugees in their own country. In the end, there were two new nations: India, with its heavily Hindu population, and Pakistan, which instantly became the most populous Muslim state in the world.

Gandhi had hoped to maintain India as one country. But with thousands of people fleeing angry mobs, this man of conscience threw his considerable political weight behind dividing the country. He began a fast in order to draw the consciousness of the Indian people toward the plight of the Muslims. He appealed to Indians to replace hatred with love. At one of his prayer meetings, Gandhi was assassinated in 1948 by a young Hindu extremist who felt that the country should not have been divided.

Gandhi's Successors

Gandhi left behind a double legacy. One was his commitment to *satyagraha*, the belief that truth and nonviolence could solve human problems. In this movement he was succeeded by Vinoba Bhave (1895–1970), who had worked beside him at Gandhi's ashram (religious community). Bhave became Gandhi's heir to the theory and practice of nonviolence. Beginning in 1951, Bhave persuaded rich landowners to donate more than 4 million acres of land, which he distributed to farmers to help them become self-sufficient.

In the political realm, Gandhi's successor was Jawaharlal Nehru (1889–1964). Nehru had been an ally of Gandhi's in the battle for Indian independence and became the new country's first prime minister, a position that he held until 1964.

Gandhi's influence was to continue long after his death and beyond the borders of India. In the United States in the 1960's, a young Baptist minister named Martin Luther King, Jr., studied Gandhi's life and philosophy. He was particularly interested in the use of nonviolence to bring about social reform. King was later to base his strategy of nonviolent protests against segregation on Gandhi's principle of *satyagraha*.

The Legacy of Reform

The modern saints of Hinduism, from Rammohan Roy to Mahatma Gandhi, had a profound influence on the religion and on Indian culture. They did much to reform the internal abuses that had crept into the religion over centuries. Due to their efforts, the government outlawed practices such as child marriage, sati, and caste-based discrimination. Although old attitudes die slowly and members of lower castes still face prejudice, it is a measure of how far India and Hinduism have come that in 1997 an "untouchable," Kocheril Raman Narayanan, was elected president. Lower caste members hailed his election as a major victory. In his address at his swearing-in ceremony, Narayanan said, "That the nation has found a consensus for its highest office in someone who has sprung from the grass-roots of our society . . . is symbolic of the fact that the concerns of the common man have now moved to the center stage of our social and political life."

Narayanan's victory also demonstrates Hinduism's ability to adapt to changing times. In Hinduism there has always been room for change. Because of the open-ended nature of the religion, saints continue to appear, and there is constant discussion and revision. Old traditions are revitalized, and if need be, new ideas are integrated and new religious societies begun. Freedom of individual thought has been intrinsically sacred to Hinduism and makes innovations possible.

The Rise of Hindu Nationalism

India is a deeply religious society, with indigenous religious and cultural traditions that go back many centuries. The modern Indian state, however, is fairly recent. Founded on democratic principles, the government of India is officially secular, that is, not linked to any specific religion. Religious minorities, which include Muslims, Sikhs, Parsis, and Christians, are supposed to be treated equally with Hindus. But secularism has never been very successful in this deeply spiritual land, where Hinduism is more than a religion. It is a culture and a way of life as well. Moreover, Hindus have never lost their mistrust of Muslims. Instead, it has grown stronger. Their feelings have led them to define themselves in opposition to "others" and to seek a deeply and uniquely Hindu identity, for themselves and for their nation.

Increasingly, the notion of what it means to be Indian has come to mean "Hindu." In part a reaction to secularism, Hindu nationalism has been on the rise since well before independence. The seeds of Hindu nationalism were sown in reform movements that urged followers to turn their backs on modernity, secularism, and other outside influences and to return to the pure Hinduism of their ancestors.

Hindutva

Hindu nationalism is built around the concept of *Hindutva*, or "Hinduness." For Hindu nationalists, Hinduism and nationalism are so closely linked as to be the same thing. An early Hindu nationalist put it like this: "A Hindu is a person who regards this land of Bharat Varsha, from the Indus to the Seas, as his Fatherland as well as his holy land that is the cradle of his religion." According to the movement, the Indian nation can only become strong through a return to its cultural roots. Nationalists define these roots as an ancient Hindu past.

Hindu nationalists feel that it is important to protect their religious and cultural traditions from secularism, which they see as an import from Western cultures and not native to India. They believe that India's religious tradition is a necessary ingredient of an Indian nation.

Hindu Nationalist Movements

The Rashtriya Swayamsevak Sangh, or RSS, is a Hindu reform movement that began in the late nineteenth century. It started as an organization of Hindu youth, with a program that included both physical exercise and moral development. From the 1940s, it has grown to become the most powerful and important Hindu nationalist organization in India.

The RSS teaches that for a nation to be successful, it must have certain "unities." These are defined as geographical unity, racial unity, religious unity, cultural unity, and unity of language. The RSS argues that the Hindus fulfilled these qualifications and were the true citizens of India. Muslims may be true citizens as well but only if they recognize the essential Hinduness of the country.

During the struggle for independence, the RSS appealed to young people who felt that Gandhi's *satyagraha* approach was too passive and gave away too much to minorities, particularly Muslims, as well as Christians and Sikhs. The government banned the RSS after the riots that lead to partition in 1948, but in 1950 the organization was reinstated and continued to gather strength. It was banned again in the early 1990s, for encouraging violence against ethnic minorities, but its influence had spread so widely that the ban could not have much effect.

Another important organization moving the country toward Hindu nationalism is the Vishwa Hindu Parishad, or VHP, an organization of religious leaders. These two organizations work to place Hinduism in the front of Indian life and thought.

Hinduism and Politics: The BJP

One way that the RSS influences daily life today is through the Bharatiya Janata Party, or BJP. Many BJP leaders came out of the RSS and have links to the VHP as well. The political goals of the BJP are frankly in harmony with those of the nationalist organizations.

Although successful in the elections of 1996 and 1998, when the BJP gained the highest number of seats but not a majority in parliament, and eventually were able to put together a coalition government, the loss in the elections of 2004 left the party searching for new leaders. During the years when the BJP led the government, it quite often put on the back burner issues related to Hindu nationalism and centered attention on economic reforms and development. It also tried to attract Muslim workers to its ranks; however, many of them abandoned the party after the 2004 elections. Even though the BJP did not push for Hindu nationalism during its reign, a large number of fundamentalist Hindus did. These fundamentalists used the official declarations of the BJP to promote communalism or the deliberate creation of conflicts between religious minorities, such as the Christians and Muslims, and the majority Hindu community. The new Congress government, with Manmohan Singh, a Sikh, as the prime minister, has been more successful at focusing attention on economic reforms. As a former financial minister of India, Singh has reenergized much of India's economy rather than handing leadership over to private groups of investors. For the time being, the accent is on economic growth rather than on any push for Hindu nationalism.

Problems of Hindu Nationalism

One of the problems Hindu nationalism has faced is that by promoting Hindu values, it has tended to harden the positions of its non-Hindu neighbors against it. Muslim Pakistan views opposition to Hindu India as a holy cause and has supported the uprisings in Kashmir, an Indian state in which Hindus are in the minority. The problems in Kashmir go back to partition. Although the population was overwhelmingly Muslim, Kashmir had a Hindu ruler. Under the partition agreement, Kashmir could have become part of either Pakistan or India, or it could have remained independent. When Pakistani troops invaded Kashmir to force its ruler to join Pakistan, he instead called on India for military protection, and the area became Indian. Kashmir's population remains mainly Muslim, and Hindus are under almost constant attack there. Many Hindus traveling to shrines in Kashmir have died at the hands of Kashmiri rebels.

Kashmir is not the only part of India in which ethnic and religious minorities have rebelled against the Indian government. To the south, Tamil separatists, who are mostly Buddhist, continue to create unrest. The Punjab, the cradle of the Sikh religion, was divided by partition, and Sikh separatists continue to agitate for a united and independent Sikh state. Both Christians and Sikhs blame the Hindu majority for human rights violations.

On the world stage, the BJP ushered India into the nuclear age by testing atomic bombs in 1998 meant as a threat to Islamic Pakistan. Pakistan retaliated by testing nuclear weapons of its own. The age-old hostilities of the Hindus and Muslims thereby took a new and more perilous turn.

Acknowledging this new reality, the United States and India signed an agreement in early 2006 (subject to approval by the U.S. Congress) that would give India access to civilian nuclear technology and allow it to continue to operate eight sites for secret military purposes. Critics have voiced concern that the agreement will undermine the Nuclear Non-Proliferation Treaty, established to stop the spread of nuclear weapons, which India has not signed.

To the north of India is its neighbor Nepal. Nepal, by its 1962 and 1990 constitutions is a Hindu kingdom, the only one in the world. The constitution guarantees religious freedom and forbids the state to discriminate among citizens on grounds of religion. With about 89 percent of the citizens of Nepal being Hindus, this is a great experiment in religious toleration for a Hindu nation. At present, Nepal is in a government crisis. King Gyanendra was running the country as an absolute monarch in an effort to prevent it from being taken over by Maoist rebels. In April 2006, however, he recalled parliament after weeks of protest against his direct rule.

CHAPTER 6

The Hindu Temple, Icons, and Worship

*T*he Hindu temple is known by many different names, three of which are *mandira* (waiting place), *prasada* (seat of grace), and *devalaya* (house of god). However, the most popular term for the Hindu temple is *mandira* (or *mandir*). The *mandira* is beiieved to be the earthly seat of a deity and the place where deities wait for their devotees. The belief that goddesses and gods dwell in the *mandira* can be traced as far back as the epics and the *Puranas.*

In later sacred texts such as the *Shastras,* special chapters were written about the building of a *mandira.* In these texts, the *mandira* is described as a crossing place where worlds of divinity and humanity meet. Hindus believe that a deity descends to Earth and takes form through sacred images located in the *mandira.* Some believe that by seeing (*Darsana*) and touching the image, it is possible to ascend temporarily to heaven and experience the divine. Although Hindus believe that God is found everywhere in the world, they also believe that their respect for the divine world, displayed in the symbolism found throughout the *mandira,* helps give shape to a divine reality that would otherwise remain formless.

In order to understand how a temple becomes a place in which deity and humankind meet, it is necessary to grasp the symbolic meaning not only of the Hindu *mandira* but also of pilgrimage centers (*tirtha sthana*), sacred images or icons (*murti*), the way of worship (*puja*), and the worshipper (*pujak*).

The Hindu *Mandira*

From the early Vedic period, Hindus have tried to create a sacred space to which gods could descend and partake of human offerings and in which people could be with the gods or ascend toward the heavens. During the later Vedic period, prayers were conveyed to the gods through sacrificial fires believed to be manifestations of Agni, the god of fire. Through fires, Vedic priests "ascended" to heaven. All such rites and ceremonies were performed in a sacred enclosure specifically prepared for communion with the gods. The tradition of this symbolic meeting of the human and the divine continues today in the Hindu *mandira*.

A *mandira* is constructed according to specific requirements. The site for a *mandira* is carefully selected. Brahmanic texts called *Shilpa Shastras,* written to direct architects and artisans, describe the requirements for such a site. One *Purana* adds to the ideas about how to build a temple in a verse about its location. It says that "the gods always play where groves are near rivers, mountains, and springs and in towns with pleasure gardens. . . . It is such places that the gods love and always dwell in."

When a site has been selected, local spirits of the land are driven away before construction begins. Then the ground is plowed, and several seeds are sown. By observing the quality of the newborn plants, the builder determines the quality of the soil. Next, the earth is smoothed until it is perfectly even, like a mirror. On this prepared land a circle is drawn, symbolizing heaven, and a square is drawn around the circle, symbolizing Earth. It is believed that the center of this circle forms a sacred pillar, connecting the "body" of the *mandira* with heaven. A small chest holding jewels and seeds and representing the essence of the temple is buried in the ground near the pillar. Above this, the innermost sanctuary, the *garbhagrah,* or "womb chamber," is constructed.

Motifs of mountains and caves are often incorporated skillfully into the architecture of the Hindu *mandira*. Throughout Hindu mythology, mountains have been depicted as sacred. Mount Kailasha in the Himalayas is the abode of Shiva; Mount Meru, like a Hindu *mandira*, is believed to be the axis of the universe, joining celestial, atmospheric, and terrestrial regions. In fact, the superstructure of a Hindu temple is called *shikhara,* meaning "the top of a mountain." Caves are also important natural symbols in Hinduism because as dark chambers with one small opening, they are believed to be symbolic of and imbued with the spirituality of the maternal womb. These chambers have traditionally served as ascetic retreats.

There are two kinds of *mandira*: rock-cut cave shrines and temples with towers. Many Hindu texts explain these symbols of cave (the inner sanctuary) and mountain (the superstructure of the *mandira*). However, during the epic and Puranic periods, the bhakti movement that emphasized devotional worship was the major influence on such temple building and the dedication of many temples to personal gods.

The earliest examples of Hindu temples were constructed around the fifth century C.E. These early stone temples were simple, columned halls covered with a flat roof. Later, this form developed into a square-columned hall raised on a flat, broad *bhumi,* or base (literally translated as "earth"), that led to the superstructure, a tower. The tower, or *shikhara* (mountain peak), was one of the most important parts of the *mandira*.

The *shikhara* rose at the rear of the *mandira*. It marked the location of the interior garbhagrah where the deity was believed to be enshrined. Divine light was believed to emit from this small, dark chamber and bless, protect, and watch over the community. Around this innermost shrine was a passageway on which devotees, moving clockwise, could encircle the inner chamber. The garbhagrah had just one opening, and only the presiding priest was allowed inside.

An assembly hall, the *mandapa,* was located in the sanctuary. This hall often led to another hall, the *natya mandapa,* where dances were performed and hymns sung to please the deities. These halls opened onto a veranda, which led to the outside.

Kalasha
head

Shikhara
peak

Pradkshana Path
*circumambulation
path*

Garbh Grah
womb chamber

Pillared Hall

Entrance

■ *This schematic
drawing represents
the essential parts of a
Hindu temple.*

The outer surface of the temple held detailed sculptures. Mythological scenes were depicted, juxtaposed with scenes from everyday life or important political events such as a royal coronation, conquests and celebrations, or portraits of royal and secular patrons. The main gateway leading toward the inner sanctuary was the only opening between sacred and profane spaces. Other openings—doors, niches, and windows—were architectural symbols of the passage of humanity to God.

The *mandira* has always been the focus of the religious, social, and cultural life of the Hindus. However, during Hindu rule it was also the political and economic center. Many features of the *mandira* have remained the same, both structurally and functionally.

By the eighth century, many freestanding temples were carved from gigantic solid stone hills. One of these was the Shiva temple at Ellora (in the state of Maharashtra). Other sacred temples with detailed mythological scenes were carved in and around immense caves, such as Elephanta (in Maharashtra) and Mahaballipuram (in Tamil Nadu). These elaborate temple complexes were sculptural and architectural marvels.

Many temple complexes resembled palace architecture. This is not surprising given that deities were considered kings. The earthly kings, who were *mandira* patrons, were considered to be divine reflections while watching over the welfare of their kingdoms. In some texts, kings were described as supports or receptacles of gods. Sometimes, kings were believed to be intermediaries between Earth and heaven, transmitting the offerings of their subjects to the celestial region and bringing back divine blessings. At times, kings were believed to be incarnations of deities or even demons, depending on the nature of their reign and protection. The royal throne was often equated with the altar, and conversely, the temple was perceived as a divine fortress from which the deities protected the world from chaos and disorder.

The *mandira* has always been a nucleus around which all artistic, intellectual, and religious life of the Hindu community was centered. Dance, music, drama, art, and architecture were integral parts of the *mandira* rituals. Thus, sacred dances and dramas were performed in the assembly halls. Mythological stories, recited earlier by bards, were enacted in the *mandira*. Worshippers sang devotional songs and recited hymns from important scriptures, such as the Vedas, the *Puranas,* and the epics.

During celebrations and festivals, money, land, or valuable objects were donated to the *mandira* by kings and rich patrons of the kingdom. Some kings in southern India celebrated battle victories or the addition of a territory to their kingdom by bestowing magnificent gifts on the *mandira*. Inscriptions on the walls of these temples describe priceless necklaces of lustrous pearls and bright coral beads, as well as gold ornaments set in precious stones. These were donated to adorn the sacred images in the temples. Utensils of pure gold were given for daily services to the deities, and metal images of the most popular divinities—Nataraja, Vishnu, Rama, Krishna, Shiva, and Parvati—were presented to the temple.

Temple building and the installation of sacred images was not only an expression of devotion and piety but also a merit-gaining act, or an act of good karma. All donor devotees were promised peace, wealth, rich harvest, and sons if they erected a temple or donated an icon. In addition, the generous gifts demonstrated physical importance and economic power to subjects and neighboring rulers.

Today, the Hindu *mandira* is considered a holy place in the midst of a profane world. As they always have been, temples and shrines are considered earthly dwelling places of the deities and a "crossing" where devotees of any caste can be with the divine reality. In a temple, worshippers believe that they can leave the world of illusion behind and approach the eternal realm of knowledge and truth.

■ Reliefs and sculptures decorate the outer walls of major Hindu temples. These works bring the mythological stories and their characters to life in exquisite detail.

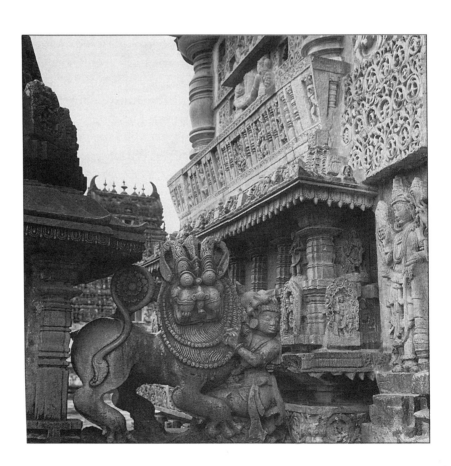

All Hindu communities have one or more local temples. Some are monumental, some are of average size, and some are quite small. Large temples are always devoted to one of the manifestations of the major deities like Shiva, Vishnu, or some form of Devi (Mahadevi Shakti). The smaller temples are devoted to minor regional deities known only to the local people. Hindus believe that they are linked with the sacred through these large temples and small shrines.

Tirtha

Like Hindu temples, *tirtha sthana* (pilgrimage centers) are crossing places of the earthly and the spiritual worlds. *Tirtha* literally means a "crossing place" or a "ford," and in a tirtha, worshippers feel closer to or even united with the deities. Journeying to a tirtha became popular because it was considered as beneficial to the pilgrim as Vedic sacrifices were to a Brahmin. Moreover, tirtha participation was accessible to devotees of all castes.

In these pilgrimage centers, worshippers have access to the mythical personages, gods, goddesses, and saints who were either born or incarnated and who performed feats of austerity at these particular sites. People travel to far-off centers because they believe that the holy places radiate sacredness for the benefit of devotees. At the holy sites, devotees feel closer to the sacred events that took place there and feel as though they were participating in the sacred history.

Several pilgrimage centers are scattered throughout India. However, four are particularly important: Badrinath in the northern Himalayas; Puri in the east; Ramesvaram in the south; and Dvarka in the west. By visiting all these sacred places one after another, in clockwise order, pilgrims encircle the holy land of India. This is just like the journey made when walking around the innermost sanctum of a *mandira*. Walking around the sanctum is considered an important ritual and a form of communion with God.

Most *tirtha sthana* are located in places that are difficult to reach. They are on the tops of mountains, deep in forests, or in the middle of deserts. Most are not accessible by modern transportation. To reach the holy destination, pilgrims need self-discipline, endurance, and devotion. A pilgrim's effort is comparable to the austerities of an ascetic, and from the act, Hindus believe that they gain spiritual merit. In addition, a person may gain status in his community after having returned from a pilgrimage.

Hindus compare their life from birth to death to a pilgrim's journey with many stations. They do not consider death as a final destination but as just one station in an endless cycle of lives. Nor do Hindus believe that death automatically brings liberation from the frustrations of life. Rather, they believe that *moksha* (final release) can be attained by complete devotion to God, knowledge of God, and through good works. Those who cannot liberate their atman (individual soul) through any of these means might attain it by completing a pilgrimage. Pilgrimage brings spiritual joy and ultimate release from the world. By visiting a *tirtha sthana,* a devotee not only re-creates and participates in sacred history by being at the site of some mythological incident—but he or she is also able to visit the temples of these places that are charged with intense sacredness.

Hindu Icons

In the Sanskrit language, a sacred statue is called *murti.* The term, which is more than 2,000 years old, refers to any figure that has a definite shape. Hindu icons, or sacred images, may be anthropomorphic—having human likeness—or they may be abstract. From the terra-cotta figurines of the Indus Valley to the modern images of Durga, all murtis are considered genuinely sacred.

The word *murti* is used in the Upanishads and the Bhagavad Gita, and it implies much more than just a simple statue. Hindu icons visually express an invisible yet fantastic divine reality. For example, the head of Nataraja, the four arms of Vishnu, Ganesha's elephant head, or Skanda's six heads are all fantastic forms depicting an incomprehensible reality. As sacred statues, these forms are easier for humankind to understand.

When icons are seen as personal deities, such as in bhakti worship, they are considered to be charged with the presence of the god. Worshipping an image is one of the ways in which a devotee can gain access to a deity. The god is invited, bathed, adorned, touched, seen, and honored in the form of the *murti*, or sacred image. Therefore, deep respect for the image of a goddess or god allows people to show their deep love for that goddess or god. Through the image, devotees can pour out their emotions to the deity.

The *Shilpa Shastras* are texts that give detailed descriptions of how a sacred image ought to be created and made suitable for the presence of a deity. The texts provide measurements of body parts, the correct posture, number of hands and heads, hand gestures (*mudras*), emblems and weapons to be held, the appropriate *vahana* (animal vehicles), suitable sitting positions (*asana*), and more. An image must be proportionate, technically correct, and pleasing to the eye. Only then do Hindus believe that it will be fit for a deity's residence. Such specific details of the gods are the result of meditation, experimentation, and extreme devotion by generations of priests and artists.

In addition to the size, shape, and artistic quality of a *murti*, there are many rituals that govern its actual making. First, whether an icon is made from wood or stone, it is important for the shilpin, or sculptor, to follow the advice of a Brahmin and cut the tree or quarry the stone at the proper time and in the proper manner. Because Hindus believe that each and every grain of matter is inhabited by local spirits, part of the ritual includes asking the spirits of the tree or rock to leave and dwell elsewhere. It is important to have a "clean" block of raw material, free of all spirits, on which to carve a divine image.

To make the icon, shilpins read about the image in the *Shilpa Shastras*. Then they focus mentally until they can form an image of the icon. Before starting the work, a ritual purification must be performed. Thus, for a traditional image maker, creating an icon is equivalent to yogic discipline in that it requires intense meditation.

When an image is completed, special rites of blessing take place. The image is purified with a variety of ritual substances such as clarified butter, honey, and a special kind of grass. In particular, the eyes of the deity are sealed with the honey and butter. Then a priest installs various deities in different parts of the body of the icon by touching its individual parts. With this ritual,

■ Ganesha, the elephant-headed son of Shiva, is the god of beginnings. Devotees worship him in order to overcome difficulties in completing a task. Ganesha blesses devotees and removes obstacles.

a particular icon may be symbolically inhabited by a number of gods other than that which it depicts. Having many gods in one recalls the one body of the Vedic Primal Man (*Purusha*) and the deities created from it in the Vedic hymn "Purusha Shukta."

Finally, breath is infused into the image through a rite called *pratishtha*, meaning "establishing the breathlike." During this rite, a special *mantra* (secret verse) is uttered. Then, the eyes are opened with a golden needle. After the blessing, the icon is considered suitable for the deity to descend into it. Most of the images are established in this manner to invoke the presence of a deity. Without the complex rituals of purification and the rites of establishment, icons are plain works of art with no sacred power.

Icons of a deity rarely show the god in one form. Rather, gods and goddesses are shown in their numerous manifestations. For instance, Shiva is depicted as Nataraja or with Parvati. Vishnu is shown in his various incarnations—Krishna, Rama, Kali, and others. Krishna and Durga are sculpted as slaying their enemies in violent and terrifying postures.

■ *The center of attention during the **Durga Puja** celebration is the image of the goddess **Mahisha mardini**, "the slayer of the demon Mahisha." Each year, at the end of the celebration, the image of the goddess is immersed in water.*

A *mandira* has movable and immovable *murtis*. Immovable images are part of the temple architecture, whereas movable images can be taken out during festival days to allow devotees to "see" the deities. Darsana, or seeing images of deities, becomes a significant act, whether the deity is at home, at the temple, or journeying in a procession. This rite of seeing is one of the basic components of Hindu worship.

Puja

Daily worship, or *puja*, is an important ritual in the lives of practicing Hindus. The daily rituals performed in the *mandira* are thought to be a source of prosperity and good health for the worshipper. The goal of *puja* is reminiscent of the Vedic fire sacrifice, in which gods were invited from the heavens and presented with different offerings. *Puja* is the most frequently performed Hindu ritual.

Vedic people believed that deities lived in the heavens. By the epic period, it was believed that divine power came to Earth if a sacred area was made ritually pure, icons were consecrated, and the deity was persuaded with verbal chants to descend. Then the god or goddess was given constant love and honor. This was because the early Hindus believed that if proper devotion and care were given to the invited deity, it would stay in the temple and watch over the community. If proper care of the images was not taken, and if the icons were not protected from vandalism and abuse, the deity would abandon it and the temple.

The idea of constant attention to a deity made it necessary for a daily routine of rituals. This resulted in the development of the Hindu *puja*. In each *mandira*, a resident priest makes sure that at sunrise, noon, sunset, and midnight the proper *puja* is performed. In addition, the priest resides in the temple so that continuous care may be taken and the god will always be present.

Visiting a *mandira* every day or even regularly is not mandatory for Hindus. Many devout Hindus keep in touch with their deities through worship at home. However, some rituals cannot be performed at home, and a priest's assistance is needed.

Puja is not congregational worship but an individual offering to a deity or to a deity and his or her companion. Reasons for temple worship could be related to personal or family health, wealth, education, general blessings, or safety. Many strive for good karma or liberation (*mukti*). Present-day rituals of *puja,* at home and in the temple, have not altered much from what was practiced during the earliest periods, although the ancient rituals have been greatly simplified.

Puja consists of three ritual steps: first, seeing the deity (Darsana); second, *puja,* or worship, which includes offering flowers, fruits, and cooked food called *bhog;* and third, retrieving the blessed food, called prasada, and consuming it. By these sacred acts, Hindus create a relationship with the divinity through their emotions and senses. As one scholar writes, "The temple is the monument of [divine] manifestations. The devotee who comes to the temple to look at it, does so as a seer, not as a mere spectator."

In their homes, most Hindus keep a shrine dedicated to one or more deities. The shrine contains images of the family deity, major gods and goddesses, saints, and ancestors. It is kept in a sacred area, which may be a corner of a room, a niche, a shelf of a cabinet or, in an affluent household, a small room set aside solely for this purpose. Other ritual paraphernalia include a container of water for sprinkling and purifying the area, a bell, a lamp to be waved in front of the deity, an incense burner, and a tray with flowers, fruit, and freshly cooked food. At the household shrine, Hindus offer a simple daily *puja.*

During the *puja,* the head of a Hindu household invites the goddess or god to descend and be present at the ceremony. When the divine presence is felt, worshippers consider that the deity has entered the *murti,* and they offer it a seat, wash its feet, and give water to it. An image might be symbolically bathed, then clothed in new garments, and embellished with ornaments. Perfumes and ointments are often applied; flowers and garlands are placed before it. Incense is burned, and a burning lamp is waved in front of the deity. Foods such as cooked rice, fruit, butter, and sugar are offered. Family members bow before the image, sip the blessed water, and receive a portion of the cooked food, which, having been blessed by the deity, is now considered sacred food for the devotees. Finally, the deity is asked to rest or depart.

In the home, the deities are invited to descend. In the *mandira*, on the other hand, they are "awakened," because in the temple, the divine guests are in their earthly home. The gods are believed to dwell in the *mandira* as royalty. At the *mandira*, full *puja* is performed several times every day. It differs from the daily *puja* performed at a home more in scale than in substance. In the temples that enshrine major Brahmanic gods, priests who celebrate full *puja* are referred to as Brahmins. Smaller temples and shrines of minor deities may be presided over by a member of a lower caste.

The light within a *mandira* is dim, caressing the eye of a devotee who may have come in from bright light. The *mandapa* (assembly hall) is charged with the scent of flowers, burning oil lamps, and incense. A devotee walks slowly toward the innermost sanctuary of the deity with the ingredients for *puja*, which may include flowers, fruit, and cooked *bhog*. Near the sanctuary, these things are handed to the priest, who then performs *puja* on behalf of the worshipper.

After seeing the image and receiving the prasada, or sacred food, the devotee walks around the passageway of the sanctuary. The ritual of *pradikshana*—encircling the womb chamber clockwise and touching the outer walls of the innermost sanctuary—is an important part of the *mandira* ritual that cannot be performed at home. Walking around an image, the inner sanctum, or the *mandira* itself is a way of paying respect to the deity, for movement is considered an important part of *puja*.

In addition to prayers and offerings, Hindu worship includes an understanding of the godly image, an experience charged with religious meaning. This experience is encouraged by the ancient act of "seeing." It is not only the worshipper "seeing" the image but also the deity "seeing" the worshipper that is considered a favorable act. This act is called Darsana. For this reason, Hindu images have strikingly large eyes to facilitate the "exchange of glances" between devotee and deity.

Similarly, in *puja* one does not only see but also touches and hears. All the senses are given special significance in *puja*. One observes the offering of the lighted lamps, touches the ritual objects and feet of the deity (where possible), hears the ringing of the bells and the sacred texts being recited, smells the incense, and tastes the blessed food offered at the end of the ritual.

The Worshipper

A Hindu worshipper, or *pujak*, may perform daily *puja* at home and on special days in the *mandira*. *Pujaks* must be physically healthy as well as ritually clean before starting to worship. They must take a bath, wear fresh clothes, and free their minds of any impure thoughts. A priest must also be physically and ritually clean. Through purifying acts, priests and worshippers are able to identify themselves with the divine object of worship.

In worship, devotees see divine images and mythological scenes on the outer walls of the *mandira*. These help the worshippers to recall all the sacred stories they have heard about or read.

With their minds full of the stories and their senses full from worship, devotees believe that they come to know that which is unknowable. Through art, architectural forms, and devotion, the worshipper can find new spiritual meaning in things.

The doorway of the *mandira* is believed to be vulnerable to the evils of the outside world. Therefore, minor divinities such as door guardians and images of sacred rivers are carved on or placed near lintels and doorjambs. These images are thought to cleanse devotees of any mental or physical impurities. They also bestow divine blessings on them as they enter the *mandira*.

Inside the *mandira*, worshippers are said to move toward the divine. They walk through a series of enclosures that become increasingly more sacred. As a person passes through these enclosures, he or she is gradually raised from an earthly level to a sacred level.

In the *mandira*, the worshippers do not physically ascend to heaven. However, by focusing spiritually, they may gain a divine enlightenment. From open spaces they reach closed spaces; from light they enter darkness; from the complexity of the world they move to the simplicity of the divine. In the final stage, the worshippers approach the doorway of the *garbhagrah* (womb chamber) and hand their offerings to the priest, who then conducts *puja* for them. The devotee waits outside, following the movements of the priest.

A common part of Hindu worship is the gestures of humility such as bowing, kneeling, lying prostrate, and the touching of feet. Honor and affection are expressed by doing for the god what one does daily for cherished family members. Family activities such as waking, bathing, dressing, cooking, serving, and sleeping become refined by daily practice. Hindu *puja* consists of doing these day-to-day activities to honor personal gods. Mundane daily acts, when refined, become ritual acts fit to be performed for the family deity. Finally, at the special time of *puja*, the god is invited, bathed, adorned, touched, seen, and honored. The secular feelings become charged with sacred intensity. Human feelings become divine love. Thus the family relationships and ritual acts of *puja* are closely interwoven. Routine chores become sacred rites when performed in honor of a deity.

CHAPTER 7

Social Duty and Rites of Passage

Dharma, meaning moral duty or law, is an important term in Hinduism. The origin and meaning of this word goes back as far as the Vedic period, when the word *rita* meant cosmic order. According to the divine law of rita, all things in the world have a proper place, function, and order. This creates a balance in the universe.

In Vedic times, cosmic order included the duty to be moral. In the *Shastra* texts, the idea of rita branched into the diverse concepts of dharma. In those texts, dharma meant not only cosmic law and moral duty but also social, ethical, and religious duty. *Shastras* emphasize that the reality of the universe depends on the proper behavior of the people. An improper action, that is, *adharma*, can lead to the fall of the universe into unreality and eventually into nothingness. Therefore, in order to maintain the universe and enhance cosmic harmony, proper behavior is necessary. Dharma, then, is responsible for the maintenance of the Hindu world.

In Hinduism, the moral and social duties of dharma are tied to the theories of karma, samsara, and ultimately, *moksha*. Therefore, it is important to learn about these three terms before

discussing Hindu *varnasramadharma*, a system of duty or law that includes the four castes and the four stages of life.

Origins of Dharma

The ideas of ethical behavior and moral life come from sacred Hindu literature. Traditionally, Hindu literature has been divided into two classes. One class is *shruti* (what is heard), covering the Vedas and Upanishads. The other is *smriti* (what is remembered), covering the epics and the *Puranas*. The *smriti* literature also includes a new literary form called sutras.

The sutras provided moral teachings. The word *sutra* literally means "a thread," and its content was to be memorized in addition to the Vedas. The earliest of the sutras were the *Griha Sutras* (domestic rituals) and *Surata Sutras* (priestly rituals). The last of the series were compositions called *Dharma Sutras* (ways of moral behavior).

The sutras were written by the Brahmins before the beginning of the present era. It perhaps seemed to the later Vedic Brahmins that one's religious life should be concerned with more than rituals—their texts describe how leading an ethical life is an integral part of religious life. The Brahmins do not deny that the rituals are sacred, but they stress the importance of ethical behavior, give instructions in social duty, and teach sacred morality. Their texts were called *Dharma Sutras.*

The Dharma Sutras were difficult to understand. Therefore, these texts were explained and expanded into compositions called *Dharma Shastras.* The shastras were written in verse, and they were easier to memorize and grasp than the Dharma Sutras. Eventually, Hindus turned to the *Dharma Shastras* as guides to ideal social behavior.

The most influential of all the *Dharma Shastras* was written by a sage named Manu. This text, written some time between 200 B.C.E. and 200 C.E., is known as the *Laws of Manu*. The *Laws of Manu* seems to have established the public norm of today's Hindu society.

The *Dharma Shastras* say that those who support dharma gain fame while alive and incomparable happiness after death. To support dharma is to behave in an ethical manner. The term

■ *Preceding page—A wedding ceremony (vivah) includes many symbolic gestures that indicate the newlyweds' new responsibilities. This charming gesture expresses the wife's new obligation to feed her husband.*

dharma, therefore, is closely related to the idea of karma—that one's actions in the present determine the conditions of one's life in the future.

Karma and Samsara

Originally, any correct activity or properly performed ritual was called karma. However, later religious philosophers expanded the meaning of this term. It came to mean that one's present actions determine one's future life. Thus, underlying the Hindu law of karma is the idea that a person's behavior leads to an appropriate reward or punishment.

Some scholars think that the idea that a future life depended on previous behavior must have developed from a long period of keenly observing plants, trees, and fields. These scholars believe that the early Hindus noted that land "gives birth" repeatedly if healthy seeds are sown and tended. They saw that plants do not really die; the death of a plant is a process by which it renews itself in the spring. In a sense, each life of a plant ends in a death in order to be reborn. A plant's regrowth is determined by the healthy or unhealthy conditions of former births. Scholars believe the early Hindus felt the same to be true of all living things.

During the Vedic period, proper ritual performance was called karma. In that era, if a priest performed certain rituals correctly he was believed to control the gods. Later, Upanishadic seers taught our current understanding of karma. They believed that all physical and mental activity was a reflection of greater cosmic processes. They taught that a person becomes good through good actions and bad through bad actions. Through these seers, the concept of the cycles of life, death, rebirth, and redeath was reinforced. These cycles were called samsara.

The theories of karma and samsara provide Hindus with a reason for human differences. If people are of differing social classes or physical and mental abilities, it must be a result of their deeds in this life or a past life. Karma and samsara also encourage Hindus to act ethically, because if they do not, they will suffer for their poor actions in the future.

The samsara cycles are an ever-changing universe of requirements, consequences, and conditions. This universe contrasts with the unconditioned and eternal world of the gods. The goal of practicing Hindus is to liberate themselves from constantly changing samsara—to find release from the cycles of rebirths and redeaths and gain existence in the realm of the gods.

Moksha

Moksha is the release from the conditional and temporary existence of this world. It is a religious state for which every Hindu strives. *Moksha* cannot be gained by action aimed at achieving something in this world. Rather, the person who wants liberation from life—*mukti*—seeks to experience the oneness of atman-Brahman, the union of one's self with the Ultimate Reality.

Moksha is not a Vedic concept. The Vedic texts are concerned with enjoyment of earthly bounties. Vedic people were awed by natural powers. They composed and chanted hymns to appease the personifications of natural forces and invite these personified gods to share the bounties of the earth. Vedic people did not want release from the good earthly life.

In Indian thought, the notion of *moksha* appeared as early as the oldest Upanishad. The term *moksha* is mentioned sometime during the sixth century C.E., and the concept is elaborated on in the epic *Mahabharata* and the *Dharma Shastras.*

A Hindu is supposed to model his life according to the dharmic norm prescribed in the *Laws of Manu*. He or she must obey caste laws and follow the stages of life. If the person leads an ideal life, as described in the sacred text, he or she will achieve liberation. This ideal Hindu life is reflected in the model of varnasramadharma.

Varnasramadharma

Varnasramadharma is a term that combines three separate words: *varna,* meaning the social caste system; *ashrama,* meaning the stages of life; and *dharma,* which means duty, law, or proper behavior. Varansramadharma is based on reciprocal social obligations. It was described in *Dharma Shastras* as a guide for male members of the Hindu community. Later, it became a system for Hindu society in general. Varnasramadharma and samsara give moral, ethical, and social values to members of the Hindu community and form the basis of the Hindu society.

The system of *varnasramadharma* was stimulated by the coming of outsiders. It was created to keep foreigners away from the core of society. It also served to organize the diverse occupations of Hindus and make a householder's position strong. This model evolved by combining two social ideals. The first is that of *varna*, the four hierarchical castes (Brahmins, Shatriyas, Vaishyas, and Shudras). The second is that of *ashrama*, or the male member's four stages of life—*brahmachari* (student), *grahasthin* (householder), *vanaprasthin* (forest dweller), and *sanyasin* (ascetic).

Varnasramadharma is a guide to living with the laws of dharma and karma. Within this system, Hindus support one another by performing the duties of their particular *varna*. Hindus believe that if one person does his or her duty imperfectly, it harms the entire society and thus the universe as a whole. One person's dharma, or duty, cannot be performed by another. As the Bhagavad Gita says, "It is better to perform one's own obligations poorly than to do another's well."

As a general rule, all the important Hindu texts assert that people, regardless of their age and occupation, should observe some common moral obligations. For example, everyone must tell the truth, practice goodwill, be forgiving, and exercise patience at all times. Such rules, in addition to varnasramadharma, are called *sanatana* (eternal) or *sadharana* (pertaining to everyone). Hindus commonly call their religion *Sanatana Dharma*.

These ideals of the four castes (see page 12) and the four stages of life (see pages 12–13) were set forth in the Hindu texts. But in practice, not many men went beyond the stage of householder. However, the possibility was open for a householder to pursue the life of a forest dweller in order to achieve *moksha*.

Varna

The idea that the world is balanced when it is made up of distinct social classes, or castes, is rooted in the Vedic hymn "Purusha Shukta":

> *When they divided the Man [Purusha]*
> *into how many parts did they divide him?*
> *What was his mouth, what were his arms,*
> *What were his thighs and his feet called?*

The Brahmin was his mouth,
of his arms was made Ksatriya,
his thighs became the Vaishya,
of his feet the Shudra was born.

The *Laws of Manu* affirm that this Vedic hymn is the Hindu justification for its social system—*varna.* The hymn refers to social divisions believed to be typical of the Aryans who immigrated to the Indus Valley and eventually to the Ganges plains. These were the Vedic people. We do not have any historical record that defines *varna* as such, but it appears from the Vedic hymns that the social system was composed of four major subdivisions—the Brahmins, the priestly class; Shatriyas, nobles or warriors; Vaishyas, the merchants and farmers; and Shudras, the servant class.

As time passed, this system became very complex. A person's duty varied according to his caste and to the stage of life he or she was passing through. Moreover, an individual's sex, family, and region further complicated the matter.

At present, the *varna* system has developed into *jatis* (subcastes) because of intercaste and interracial marriages. When members of the same caste married, the same caste continued for the next generation. When members of different castes married, their offspring generated a new caste. This new generation belonged to a caste lower than the three upper castes, but higher than Shudra (the lowest). However, if a member of any of the three upper classes married a Shudra or a member of any other race, their children were "untouchables." These children belonged to a class lower than the Shudras. This complicated system resulted in the creation of thousands of jatis.

Hindus belonging to these *jatis* live throughout India. They have rules governing marriage, food, occupation, and other activities. This is done to keep family purity. Punishment for disobeying the rules of marriage results in expulsion from the *jati* to which one belongs.

For many Hindus, the *jatis* are simply subdivisions of the classical *varna.* Belonging to a particular *varna* through their *jati* is important because they believe that it plays a part in the reward or punishment each soul receives for its actions during a previous existence. For Hindus, present life conditions have something to do with the purity and sanctity of Brahmins and the high or low rank attributed to each *jati*. However, social caste is believed to be due mainly to the life led by a soul in its previous incarnations. Brahmins are supposed to have the purest souls. If a Brahmin is wicked, however, he may be reborn as a member of a much lower caste or even as an untouchable as punishment.

The four varnas make up a workable system that depicts all members of society supporting one another. Brahmins, at the top of the system, were formerly required to teach the Vedas, assist in sacrifices, and accept gifts. No other caste under any circumstances could perform these three duties. The top priority of the Brahmins was maintaining the purity of their class for the purpose of domestic and temple rituals. Vegetarianism was encouraged and eventually became a norm among Brahmins. Thus, Brahmins who "were not desirous of killing" retained their higher rank.

Shatriyas were rulers and warriors. As kings, they had power on Earth. They protected their subjects and looked after the proper functioning of the society. As warriors, their caste duty was to slay enemies. Vaishyas, on the other hand, had the duty of breeding cattle. In addition, they were agriculturists and moneylenders. Along with Brahmins and Shatriyas, they could study the Vedas, perform sacrifices, and offer sacred gifts. Moreover, they, too, participated in the rites of passage and wore the sacred thread. However, the Vaishyas were not permitted to perform religious rites or the duties of a warrior.

Shudras performed only minor sacrifices and simplified domestic rituals that did not require reciting from the Vedas. They did all sorts of manual work so that society as a whole could function smoothly. They were not permitted to perform any sacred rituals. Furthermore, they were not officially initiated into the system of varnasramadharma, although they took care of the basic necessities of the society.

Ashrama

During the sixth century, the idea of a life of celibacy and renunciation was sweeping the Ganges river valley. New religions, such as Buddhism and Jainism, had branched away from the Vedic tradition. Considering that human beings were bound to endless cycles of samsara, common people questioned the value of Vedic sacrifices. What was the purpose of the Vedic sacrificial ritual done in order to appease gods? If humans were bound to samsara no matter what, how was sacrifice going to help?

During this fertile period of varied religious growth, Brahmins attempted to find theological justifications for their way of thinking so that their members would not convert to other religions. They wanted to find a religious way that would make the life of ascetics and renouncers acceptable in the mainstream of their own religion, while still maintaining the religious importance of marriage, ritual sacrifice, and other Vedic institutions. One of their solutions was the system of the *ashramas,* which became one of the most significant of the sacred laws.

Ashramas are viewed as the four rungs in the ladder leading up to liberation, or *moksha.* Although the student stage is the time for preparation for adult life, the householder stage is the most important stage in this system. The forest dweller and ascetic stages are regarded as belonging to the time of old age and retirement. Persons situated in each *ashrama* are expected to pay respect to those who belong to a higher stage than they do.

Brahmachari, the Student

As a student, or *brahmachari,* a Hindu male was to study diligently in order to know the sacred traditions and literature. Between the ages of eight and 12, a boy of any of the three upper castes could study the Vedas after he was initiated by a teacher who had accepted him as a student. The boy went through a rite of initiation before he was allowed to live with his teacher. Once accepted, he was instructed in the recitation of the sacred texts.

In the teacher's ashram, the student lived a life of poverty and submission. He was supposed to live as a personal servant of the teacher and do all of his teacher's daily chores, such as toting fuel and water, serving food, and cleaning up. He was expected to show great devotion and respect to his teacher. He completed his studies after several years of living in this manner.

Grahasthin, the Householder

When the young man completed his studies, he was expected to marry. This was considered the second *ashrama,* that of grahasthin, the householder. The man was expected to earn a living for himself, beget sons, and take care of his family by doing work appropriate to his caste. In addition, he was expected to give alms to those who had passed into the higher *ashrama,* that of the forest dweller and ascetic.

Marriage and begetting sons were immensely important in this *ashrama.* The relationship between husband and wife is described in the *Dharma Shastras.* As long as the wife lived, she was not to do anything to displease her husband. After his death, she was to remain devoted to his memory and was never to even utter the name of another man.

Vanaprahsthin, the Forest Dweller

When a man had fulfilled his duties as the head of the family, when his skin was wrinkled and his hair white, he was expected to leave his home and community and proceed toward the higher *ashrama—vanaprahsthin*—that of the forest dweller. The forest dweller contributed to the welfare of the society by performing rituals in honor of his ancestors. However, only a very small percentage of people really left home in order to live in the forest away from family and community. Most people paid homage to their ancestors while living at home and went on pilgrimages each year to be closer to the gods.

Sanyasin, the Ascetic

The last *ashrama* in one's life, sanyasin, became necessary if one wished to achieve liberation. The difference between a forest dweller and an ascetic is never clearly stated in Hindu texts. Perhaps seclusion from family and community for a period of time, that is, living the life of a forest dweller, was essential before one could completely give up the world, physically as well as mentally.

It was only at this fourth stage that one could understand the mystery of the divine, experience its presence, and possibly have communion with it. A forest dweller who was not a *sanyasin*

■ *Sadhus (holy men) are a common sight in India. These two Sadhus belong to two different sects of Hinduism, as indicated by the marks on their foreheads. Generally speaking, horizontal lines indicate Vaishnava affiliation, and vertical lines indicate Shaiva affiliation.*

could keep in touch with the world in general, but the ascetic stayed completely away from it. Living his life with only the most basic personal items, he had no physical comfort. His whole day was devoted to meditation, reflection, and the reading of Upanishadic scriptures. It was believed that this simple yet serene state of the *sanyasin* continued beyond death and that such people never returned to this world. Such ascetics are esteemed in Hindu society and are entitled to special respect and support.

Ashramas and varnas form two pillars of the Hindu social and family systems of the *Sanatana Dharma*. Besides teaching the significance of the caste system and four stages of life, the sacred texts of the Brahmanic tradition also describe some rituals that should be performed at strategic points in a Hindu's life.

Rites of Passage

Rituals performed and celebrated at the time of important transitions in the life of a Hindu, from the moment of conception to the time of death, are called *samskara*. There are four major rites of passage, passed down in the mainstream Brahmanic tradition and described in the shastras. These are the prenatal, childhood, marriage, and death rituals.

On such occasions, family members and friends join together to bless the individual and to protect him or her from any harm. All major rituals are performed at home. Family priests are usually called in to perform the most important rituals, but family members are usually the primary performers of the home rituals.

Prenatal Rituals

Three rites are performed before the birth of a child: the rite of conception, the wish for a male child, and protection of the fetus. To ensure the fertility and safety of the mother and child, the rite of conception is performed long before there is any news of the arrival of a child. In the third or fourth month of pregnancy, a rite is performed for procuring a male child. This ceremony also contains rites and safeguards against miscarriages. Finally, between the fourth and the eighth month of pregnancy, a rite is performed to protect the fetus from evil spirits.

Childhood Rituals

A number of rituals are performed between a child's birth and adolescence. The first is a simple ritual, performed immediately after birth. The most important is the second ritual, known as the naming ceremony, which is held on the 10th or 12th day after the birth of the baby. On this occasion, the baby is given a formal name. The third ritual is celebrated when a baby is weaned from its mother and given solid food to eat for the first time. This is celebrated sometime in the sixth month. Between the ages of one and five, girls experience a ceremonial ear piercing, and the boys have their first haircut. These two ceremonies conclude the childhood rites.

Many of the childhood and adolescence rituals are aimed at protecting and nurturing the child. However, others have social significance. Through them, the young child is prepared to assume the social and religious responsibilities of the adult world.

The main ritual of adolescence is the Vedic initiation rite called *upanayana* (popularly known as the "thread ceremony"). It is regarded as the second birth of the initiate. Only male children of the upper three castes (Brahmins, Kshatriyas, and Vaishyas) go through this ceremony of initiation into their respective classes.

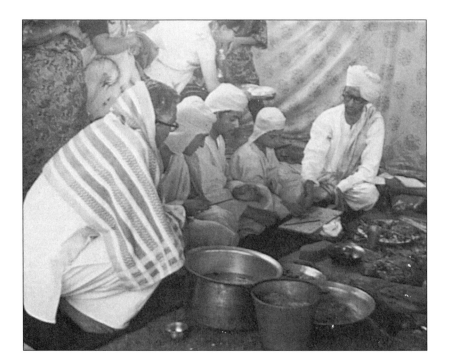

■ *Three brothers prepare for the elaborate rite of passage called* **upanayana,** *the "thread ceremony." Priests and family members are present at the ceremony, which is performed in front of a fire pit.*

Males who take part in the *upanayana* ritual are called "twice born" because they are spiritually reborn at this ceremony. Their first birth, from their mother's womb, is considered incomplete. At the *upanayana* ceremony, the children are "born again" as members of the Hindu social system. Members of the fourth caste, Shudras, do not go through this ceremony. Therefore they are born only physically, not spiritually, and for this reason they are not considered pure. Thus, they are not fit to do any work that is considered sacred. Before the ritual of initiation, the children of higher classes are considered the same as Shudras. Men of the three higher castes who remain uninitiated after the ages of 16, 22, and 24, respectively, are regarded as impure, and social interaction with them is forbidden.

Before the ritual of *upanayana*, the boy eats his last meal with his mother. From that moment, he is expected to eat with the adult male members of his family. His head is then shaved, and he is bathed. He wears a girdle of deerskin (nowadays replaced by cotton material), carries a wooden staff, and is given finally the Sacred Thread. This thread, or *upavita*, consists of three cords, each of which is made by twisting three strands. The *upavita* is a visible symbol of all individual existences, inseparable and linked to one single source of the universe. The thread is normally worn over the left shoulder and hangs under the right arm. It is regarded as the central component of the initiation rituals.

After the completion of this ceremony, the young man, along with the priest, puts wood into the sacred fire. This is the boy's first encounter with the sacrifice, the central religious act of the Vedic religion. Formerly, the pupil remained for many years after the ceremony at the teacher's house, away from his own home and family. During this time he had no status, rank, or property. Rather, he led a life of humility, obedience, and chastity. In present times, many young men perform this ritual before they go to college, or even later, before they get married. Modern young men do not live with the teacher unless they have decided to devote their lives to the study of scriptures.

At the completion of his studies, another ritual incorporates the student into society. In modern times, this ritual takes place when a child graduates and returns to his parents' home. The central theme of this ritual is a ceremonial bath. After the bath, the student becomes a full-fledged member of the community. He is ready to marry and become a householder. The search for a suitable bride begins.

Marriage

Marriage (*vivah*) is one of the most important rituals in the life of a Hindu. Only a married man is allowed to perform principal religious sacrifices. In addition, he is the only one who takes care of family members belonging to all four *ashramas* of life (unmarried men are responsible only for relatives who belong to the first two ashramas). Thus, a married man's role is pivotal in Hindu society. However, such a man is considered complete only after begetting a son.

The first step in the *vivah* is finding a suitable match. The parents make their choice with the child's consent. Then, with the help of an astrological calendar and the family priest, they decide on a favorable day for the marriage ritual.

The betrothal takes place some time before the day of the marriage. On the wedding day, the groom goes to the bride's house in a colorful procession along with many friends and relatives. The bride wears bright red attire, symbolizing love and faith, and the groom wears white traditional dress, symbolizing purity and serenity. The father of the groom asks for the bride's hand, and the bride's father formally offers it. The marriage ritual is conducted by a family priest belonging to the Brahmin class. Although the main ritual varies from region to region, the four basic rites remain the same and form the core of the ceremony.

The rites are performed in front of a fire pit made of bricks. The priest sits close to the fire, Agni, with the bride, the groom, and the parents of the bride and groom. The invited family and friends encircle this group while the priest performs the wedding rites. In the wedding ritual, as in *puja*, bells are rung, the Vedic hymns are chanted, and fragrant flowers, clarified butter, uncooked grain, and many other such ingredients are poured as oblations into Agni.

Amid the festive sounds, sweet smells, and vibrant colors, the bridegroom says to the bride that he will take care of her health and happiness. He then guides her three times around the fire. After each complete turn, he recites a mantra. He tells her, "Be my friend. May you be devoted to me. Let us have many sons. May they reach old age." Then the couple takes seven steps around the fire. The taking of the seven steps is the most important part of the ceremony. To symbolize their union, the bride and the groom eat a common meal while sitting together. After the marriage ritual, the couple goes to the husband's home, and on the fourth day, several rites are performed to ensure fertility.

Cremation and the Last Rites

When someone dies, family and friends are quickly informed. Within a few hours, the dead body is carried on a litter in a procession to the local cremation ground. The procession is led by the eldest son, acting as the chief mourner of the deceased. The name of a god—either Rama, *Hari* (Krishna), or Shiva—is cried out as the procession moves. At the cremation ground, the body is laid on a specially prepared pyre of wood and is cremated in the belief that its soul will be united with the ancestors after the proper funerary rituals are performed. The mourners return to their homes without looking back.

Cremation has been the customary way of taking care of human remains since the earliest period of Indian history. Cremation was regarded as the last sacrifice, *antyesti*, in which one's own body is offered in the sacred fire, Agni. It is believed that from the fire the deceased person is born again into a new existence in the company of his or her ancestors.

The funerary ritual, *sraddha*, is performed in order to help the deceased reach the homes of the ancestors safely. It is believed that after the cremation, the people who have died pass through a period when they live as ghosts. During this period, which may last as long as one year, they are dangerous, and their relatives are impure. Offerings of food and water are made for the newly deceased in the ritual of sraddha. Balls of rice and libations of water are offered, accompanied by the recitation of texts expressing respect and concern. The death rituals are the rites of passage from the earthly existence to the world of the fathers. They last anywhere from 12 days to a year, depending on the beliefs of the person who is performing them.

One notices a remarkable feature in all the rites of passage of Hindus—they do not refer at all to the common Hindu belief of karma, samsara, and *moksha*. These rites are founded on a world-view that celebrates life and fertility, and when death inevitably arrives, Hindus ritually transport the dead to the world of the fathers. A significant element that is consistent from the Vedic sacrifices to the contemporary Hindu rituals is the role of fire as a central element of almost all the rites of passage.

The prenatal, childhood, marriage, and death rituals are also performed for women belonging to the twice-born castes. During these times, Vedic formulas are not recited, since women are not allowed to read or hear the Vedas. Indeed, within the system of *varnasramadharma*, women were not believed to be spiritually inclined. They did not enter into any of the stages of life, they were dependent on their fathers as young girls, on their husbands as women, and in their old age, they were the responsibility of their sons.

■ **Months of the Hindu Lunar Calendar**

Chaitra	March/April
Vaishakha	April/May
Jyaishtha	May/June
Ashadha	June/July
Shravana	July/August
Bhadra	August/September
Ashvina	September/October
Kartika	October/November
Agrahyana (Margasiasa)	November/December
Pausa	November/December
Magha	January/February
Phalguna	February/March

Shukla Paksha is the fortnight of the waxing moon. **Krishna Paksha** is the fortnight of the waning moon.

CHAPTER 8

Innovations and Modern Hinduism

*T*he religious life of Hindus today is devoted to bhakti, *puja*, rituals and festivals performed at home and in the temple, and the *varnasramadharma* system of duties and obligations. Some Hindus follow all of these traditions and others just a few. Thousands of modern Hindus practice another ancient tradition—that of devotion to saints. The saints have led the innovative movements in Hinduism.

The Role of the Saints

In Hinduism, saints have been pivotal in generating and spreading new ideas rooted in ancient traditions. The extraordinary saint-poets of the epics and the *Puranas* and the bhakti movement made Brahmanism available to the common people. During Islamic rule, the wandering minstrels kept Hindu beliefs and traditions alive without changing Hinduism's internal structure. During the 19th century, modern Hindus rediscovered their forgotten scriptures as they came face to face with the Industrial Revolution and Christianity. This environment led to new religious movements.